FACE TO FACE
OCEAN PORTRAITS

FACE TO FACE
OCEAN PORTRAITS

HUW LEWIS-JONES

CONWAY

Published in association with
POLARWORLD

First published in Great Britain in 2010 by Conway, an imprint of Anova Books Company Ltd, 10 Southcombe Street, London W14 ORA, in association with Polarworld.

Designed by Liz House.
Printed and bound by 1010 Printing International Ltd, China.

FRONT COVER: Stewart 'Tea-boy' Kirk, the last shore attendant for the Royal National Lifeboat Institution, Hoylake lifeboat station, 1992.

FRONT MONTAGE, pp. 6-7.
Top left to bottom right: Barracudas surround diver Dinah Halstead, Papua New Guinea, 1987; Lifeboat crewman Dougie Armitage, Hoylake station, 1992; J-class yacht *Velsheda* races at the Antigua Classic Regatta, 2001; Italian ocean rower Alex Bellini relaxes on Lake Como near Mandello del Lario, 2009; Frank Beken demonstrates his 'marine camera', 1935; Underwater film producer Michele Hall comes face to face with an octopus off Whyalla, South Australia, 2008; A young crew member of the German barque *Herzogin Cecile* encourages a Southern Royal Albatross to pose for a photograph in 1928, 'the poor thing was seasick so was let go again'; The St Davids Tyne-class lifeboat *Garside* powers through the waves, 2005; Jean-Michel Cousteau enjoys a dive with a Hawksbill turtle, Papua New Guinea, 2008; Abbey emerges from the sea, photographed using the wet-plate collodion process, 2008; Lifeboat crewman and museum keeper Frank 'Jumbo' Muirhead on the beach at Cromer, 2009; The elegant gaff-rigged cutter *Kathleen*, 1901; Syd Bensley, the mate of the Grimsby trawler *Northern Princess*, examines his net, 1952; Veteran marine explorer Don Walsh wears his old deep-sea diving helmet, 2009; The crew of the pioneering craft *Resurgam*, the world's first propelled submarine, appear shortly before its launch in 1879; David Doubilet on assignment with Caribbean reef sharks, 2008.

REAR MONTAGE, pp. 286-87.
Top left to bottom right: A crewman from the Appledore lifeboat comes to the rescue, 2005; Glaciologist Roy 'Fritz' Koerner on the Arctic Ocean, 1969; Ellen MacArthur onboard the Open 60 *Kingfisher*, during a photo shoot in the Solent, 2000; A lone swimmer heads for the bathing huts, 1907; George Watson, the watchman of HMS *Warspite* poses with the ship's cat 'Stripey' shortly before the famous battleship was scrapped, 1947; James Tomlinson explores the depths at Sunsail Antigua, 2008; A Falmouth fisherman relaxes with a pint, 1948; Norwegian explorer Thor Heyerdahl, who became world famous in 1947 when he skippered the small balsawood raft *Kon-Tiki* across the Pacific Ocean from Peru to Tahiti, is photographed in Tenerife, 1998; Veteran surfer Roger Mansfield relaxes in the sunshine on the cliff-tops above Newquay Bay, 2009; Merchant Navy engineer officer Howard Flood at home at Hawarden, Flintshire, 2009; La Jolla Shores legend Dave McLeod at the 'Gathering of the Tribes' surf contest, Church Beach, San Onofre, 2010; Ernest Shackleton at the wheel of *Nimrod* on her Antarctic voyage, 1909; A new ship's propeller, inspected in Greenwich, 1964; *Ericsson 3* makes her way in to Cape Town, after the opening stage of the Volvo Ocean Race, 2008; David Doubilet photographing Caribbean reef sharks at a wreck in waters off the Bahamas, 2008; Despite losing her left arm in a shark attack in 2003, Hawaiian surfer Bethany Hamilton bravely returned to the oceans and the sport she has loved since childhood.

REAR PAGE: 'Captain' Elvy shows off his new tattoos in 1943. 'Sailor' George Fosdick was the artist responsible for this amazing maritime work featuring mermaids, flying fish, and a clipper ship under full sail. We know next to nothing about the mariner Elvy, though he may have later worked as a circus attraction on the American west coast. With loss overboard and shipwreck a common peril of the nineteenth-century sea-faring life, sailors' appearances were logged on 'protection certificates', which even detailed their tattoos, to help with identification of their bodies. As much as decoration, the tattoo became an integral part of a mariner's identity – both in life and in death.

ISBN: 9781844861248

polarworld

www.anovabooks.com
www.conwaypublishing.com
www.polarworld.co.uk

PREVIOUS PAGE: An unidentified sailor from HMS *Prince* stops for a portrait before rejoining his ship, 1917.

RIGHT: A humpback whale cruises past in the ocean off Tonga. This enigmatic portrait, by Sue Flood, won the best single image of 'natural wonders' in the *Travel Photographer of the Year* competition, 2009.

CONTENTS

LEFT: *Ericsson 4* leaves Cape Town bound for India, at the start of Leg 2 of the Volvo Ocean Race on 15 November 2008. Spanning some 37,000 nautical miles, visiting eleven ports over nine months, the Volvo Ocean Race is the world's premier ocean yacht race for professional crews. Skippered by the masterly Torben Grael, *Ericsson 4* emerged as the overall winner.

P16-17: The *Granite State*, an American ship built in 1877, was sailing to Swansea with a cargo of wheat when she struck the Runnelstone, three miles south-east of Land's End. She was hauled off and towed, severely waterlogged, to the shelter of Porthcurno Bay, where this rare photograph was taken in November 1895. All seemed well, but when her cargo of wheat started to swell and burst her hatches, the crew had to abandon ship and take to the boats. Sightseers had only a few days to view the grounded ship before she was smashed to pieces by a savage winter storm.

P18-19: Renowned underwater cinematographer Didier Noirot leaves the security of his dive cage to come face to face with a huge great white shark in the waters off Guadalupe Island, Mexico, 2006. He has spent the last few years with Jacques Perrin filming *Oceans*, the ground-breaking wildlife documentary released in 2010. He is now working on the *Frozen Planet* series produced by the BBC and Discovery.

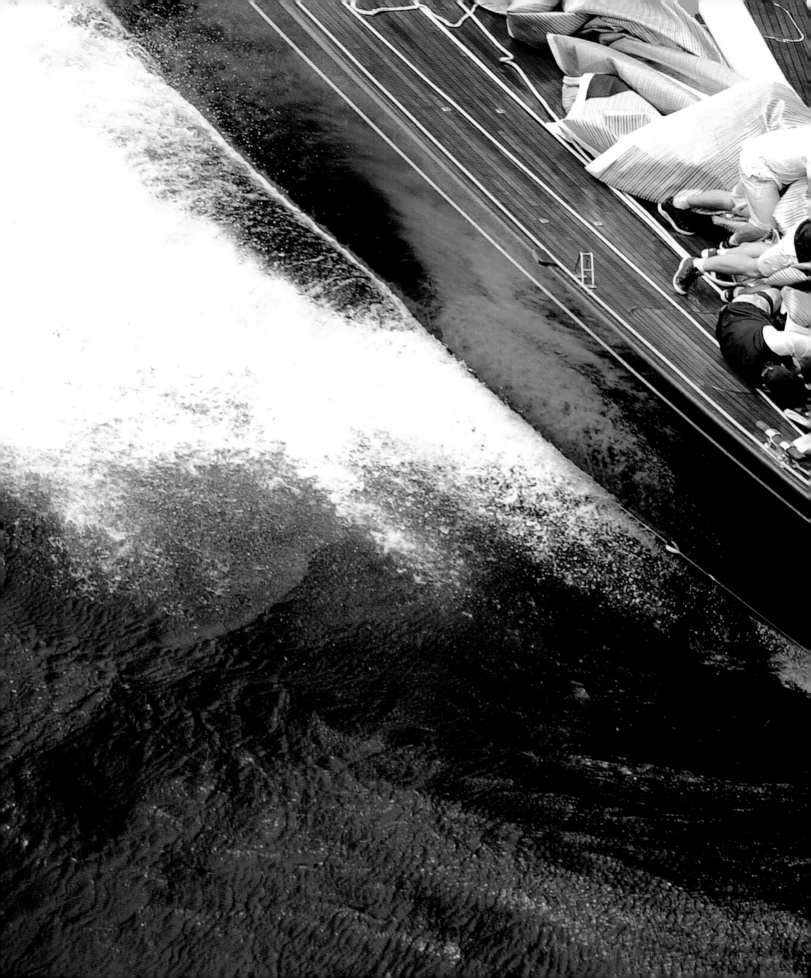

THE CALL OF THE SEA

There is nothing more enticing, disenchanting, and enslaving than the life at sea.

JOSEPH CONRAD, *Lord Jim*, 1900

Water covers more than two-thirds of the earth; man had to find his way across it. And so, down through the ages, man with his ingenuity and his courage fashioned the ship – free, charged with the strength and grace and poetry of the singing sea. And where once dugout and raft, galley and galleon, tall clipper and beamy paddle-wheeler tracked the sea, now giant freighters, tankers, and liners steam in endless movement around the world, bearing man's cargoes, his hopes, himself. But as he created the ship, the ship has shaped his course. Harbinger of civilization, agent of discovery and migration, it became the mightiest mobile creation the world has ever known.

ALAN VILLIERS, *Men, Ships, and the Sea*, 1962

The sea drives truth into a man like salt.

HILAIRE BELLOC, *First and Last*, 1911

FOREWORD

THE CALL OF THE SEA

SIR ROBIN KNOX-JOHNSTON

Forty years ago, nine men set out to be the first to sail around the world, alone, without stopping. There was no accepted ideal craft; some, like mine, were heavy cruisers, others were lightweight trimarans. I made the decision to attempt the voyage early on and watched as better-funded campaigns came along threatening my hopes of being the first. Sailing out of Falmouth with everyone either telling me the voyage was impossible, or that I was not capable of doing it, was one of those occasions when you know you have committed yourself completely. To turn back then would be to lose all self-respect and credibility. When faced with an easy or difficult choice, I've always thought it better to take the hard one because its achievement will bring real satisfaction. In any case, I was angered by the doubters. It was seen as an impossible dream, but we humans tend to turn the impossible into the possible if we really believe.

In the 1960s, I was serving in India as a merchant navy officer with the British India Steam Navigation Company, where my beloved 32-foot ketch *Suhaili*, which means 'southeast wind' in Arabic, was built. When I became due for long leave, my brother and I sailed her the 12,000 miles back to London. *Suhaili* was designed by William Atkins in 1923 and was based on Norwegian sailing lifeboat designs. She was solidly built and she needed to be.

Stocked with provisions, some spares, books, and a few essential bottles of whisky, I left Falmouth in 1968. There was no electronic navigational equipment. In some respects, I had much the same gear as Captain Cook, a sextant and chronometer. I did not even have wind instruments – I used strands of wool fastened to the rigging to give some idea of where the breeze was coming from. Within two months I had lost my radio, so from then on had no contact at all apart from infrequent sightings of ships, most of whom did not notice me, and some fishermen off the coast of New Zealand.

The solo sailor has to learn to live with isolation, sleep deprivation, the frustrations of calms, the need to trim sails to suit the changing weather. Your life

PREVIOUS PAGE: J-class yacht *Velsheda* races in the Antigua Classic Yacht Regatta, 2003. She was designed by Charles Nicholson and built in 1933 and sailed against many of the great yachts of that golden age, *Britannia*, *Endeavour* and *Shamrock*. For many years after the War she lay derelict in a mud berth on the River Hamble. She was finally restored to her racing glory in 1997.

LEFT: The *Terra Nova* battles through a violent storm in the Southern Ocean, late November 1910. Although he suffered badly from sea-sickness, Herbert Ponting continued to take a number of dramatic photographs on Scott's voyage to Antarctica. This image shows the pumps being manned during the gale: 'the seas were continually breaking over these people and now and again they would be completely submerged'.

is dominated by the boat's needs, because if she is damaged your life is threatened. In storms there is no crawling into a tent and sleeping through the howling winds, this is when the boat needs you most, caring for her, watching the approaching waves and picking a way through that most dangerous threat of all, the cross seas, when waves are coming from different directions. If the boat is right for one wave she will be wrong for the next, resulting in a knockdown, when the boat can be rammed onto her side, or further. This is when tiredness can sap the will to keep going, but to leave the boat to her own devices is probably a death sentence. You have to keep going.

But it is not always dangerous huge seas or agonising flat calms. In the trade winds the boat presses on through sparkling blue seas and you would not want to swap your place with anyone. One treasures these moments of pure beauty on the ocean, but even in good conditions the sea is notoriously hard to photograph, in bad it is almost impossible. The waves in some parts of

Though the face of maritime exploration has no doubt changed, the sea remains a hard and uncompromising master.

the world can exceed thirty metres in height, especially in the Southern Ocean. They are huge and threatening when you are amongst them, vast watery Himalayas. Often you are too busy looking after the boat to take photographs, but whenever you see pictures of a storm you were in, they always show the waves smaller and flatter than you remember. Maybe this is your memory playing up, but then, when occasionally you see videos of a storm, taken from a helicopter, then you can see how enormous waves can become.

For five months I sailed through the Southern Ocean on my little *Suhaili*. Not a racing boat, but a tough little cruiser. She was not capable of high speeds but she was capable of surviving. Nothing remained dry, clothes became so salt encrusted that it was better to drag them in the sea to reduce the density of salt in them. Fresh water came from the clouds. The conditions were not much different from the lives of the sailors on square-riggers a century before, and once my radio broke down I was as isolated as they had been. Sadly, even though I had an underwater camera, I did not use it as much as I should. The white outs, when the whole sea became white with spindrift, remained unrecorded because it was not possible to look into the wind. When a giant wave approached you were too distracted by

making sure you were as sheltered as possible and tied on to think of taking photographs with a camera that could easily be smashed or torn from your grasp if the wave swept the boat.

But if waves are hard to catch on a camera, the faces of those who spend years at sea are not. The weather-beaten features that have been formed by facing up to nature in all its raw moods reveal the honest character of those who know that you cannot fool the sea. The best media spin in the world is of no use when the sea rages. There is no escape from a storm in the middle of an ocean, no button to press to change the television channel when you don't like the programme, you have to live through it to survive however long it may last. If you don't look after your boat and nurse it through difficult times it won't look after you.

Perhaps the experience is less etched into the features of today's adventurous sailors. The challenges are very real, and modern media coverage creates a raft of new pressures, but technology nonetheless offers support, reassurance, a connection to home. Photographs trail in our wake, in fact, they are instantly beamed across the globe, giving followers a graphic account of a voyage's perils, perhaps providing fans with an update on a race, or satisfying the perfect shot for an eager sponsor. Not just still images of course, but now real-time moving pictures too, streamed by satellite, viewed easily online: the ocean within our living rooms, nature's power and beauty available to all of us on our screens, but is this enough?

A century ago ships' bridges were open, and only forty years ago there was no self-steering to keep the boat on a safe course that allowed a sailor to shelter below when things got rough, they had to be up there, in the open, at the helm. Nor were there winches to help muscles control the sheets and halliards of the sails. It created a tough, uncompromising breed, experienced in nature's sometimes vicious, sometimes benign moods. The prayer of Elizabethan captain John Davis, his crew reduced to five fit men, and still trying to get through the Magellan Strait into the Pacific, sums them up: 'Oh Lord, if we are bound to die, then I would rather have it in proceeding than retreating'.

You can glimpse these lives in fine maritime collections on both sides of the Atlantic and a haul of rare and enigmatic portraits appear here for the very first time. In creating this wonderful book, Dr Huw Lewis-Jones enables us to encounter the many generations of tough, resourceful people whose lives were bound to the sea. It is an honour to share in their

ABOVE and RIGHT: Sir Robin Knox-Johnston, one of Britain's finest yachtsmen, and the first man to sail non-stop and alone around the world, photographed by Nigel Millard, 2010.

stories. These historic treasures are matched by some of the very best in marine photography from the modern ocean world. Though there are huge differences between the types of people who 'go down to the sea' in the ships of today, there are many things that remain for us unchanged, to be experienced and enjoyed as in the past. And there are, of course, fresh challenges to face those who continue to dream about the ocean. It is hard not to feel inspired by the individuals you will meet and read about in these pages.

   Though the face of maritime exploration has no doubt changed, the sea remains a hard and uncompromising master. It obeys its own natural rules, which have to be learned by experience; rules that are not always pleasant ones. Once you have commenced a voyage you have to face what is thrown at you. There is no escape, and often little hope of rescue. But those who are prepared to live by these rules experience the freedom that comes from being in charge of their own destiny. Sealed away from society in their own small world they are free to choose their ocean and explore, knowing that it is their own decisions, no one else's, that will decide their success. Experience this liberating independence, however fleeting it is, and you find that the sea calls you for the rest of your life. No one can truly explain why we do it, or what this freedom means. But, for those of us who choose this life, it is magical, and photographs can convey some of the pleasure.

Gosport, 2010

PHOTOGRAPHY THEN

This is the pleasure of life at sea – fine weather, day after day, without interruption, fair wind, and plenty of it, and homeward bound.

RICHARD HENRY DANA, *Two Years Before the Mast,* **1840**

Travellers who are photographers, as are most people to some extent nowadays, have exceptional opportunities at sea for the exercise of their art. The clear light is an immense advantage ... photographs of clouds, waterspouts, waves and other phenomena are of much value in the study of meteorology. Pictures taken of birds in flight or at rest, or fishes and other animals swimming and jumping, may all add to our knowledge.

ALFRED CARPENTER, *Nature Notes for Ocean Voyagers,* **1915**

For sheer downright misery give me a hurricane, not too warm, the yard of a sailing ship, a wet sail and a bout of sea-sickness.

APSLEY CHERRY-GARRARD, *The Worst Journey in the World,* **1922**

ESSAY

PHOTOGRAPHY THEN

HUW LEWIS-JONES

There are many places in the world where our story might begin. We could start by accompanying two camera artists as they venture along a windswept beach in northern Scotland, in search of fisherfolk willing to sit for the very first maritime portraits. Or maybe, we arrive on the shifting deck of a wooden sailing vessel as she plys her way through the troughs of an Atlantic swell, harvesting pioneering scientific measurements to open the secrets of the deep. High above, perhaps, we join an adventurous soul swaying with his apparatus on the yardarm, desperate to secure a shot in the mighty roll of the Southern Ocean. But not yet, we shall meet these remarkable photographers soon, instead this story opens in Vienna. The year is 1800 and Admiral Nelson is sat in a chair with straws up his nose.

Some forty years before photography's arrival revolutionised the way people saw themselves, one of the most fashionable ways of securing your likeness involved a bucket of wet plaster and a great deal of patience. Exhausted by seven years of war, Nelson had been recalled from naval duty in the Mediterranean and

was travelling overland through Austrian territory, with his pregnant mistress and her husband in tow, on their way home to England. Famous for his exploits at the Battle of the Nile, he was the lion of the day. While most were satisfied with a glimpse of their hero passing in his carriage or dancing at a ball, some admirers suggested they would like his bust to decorate their parlours. Never one to step modestly from the public gaze, Nelson agreed and was ushered into the sculpture studio of Franz Thaller. During this unglamorous procedure, he was very likely strapped into a tilted chair and told to keep his eyes firmly closed. Straws were inserted into each of his nostrils, helping him to breathe while wet plaster was slopped, smothered, and then artfully moulded all over his face. He had to stay completely still until the plaster was set hard enough to remove in sections.

This simple cast was the starting point for a relentless cycle of portraits celebrating the newest ocean hero. Where once it had been the maritime exploits of Sir Francis Drake or Captain James Cook that had captured the public imagination, making them the most famous men of their day, now it was Nelson who ruled the

PREVIOUS PAGE: The crew of a Sheringham crab boat rest a while for the camera in 1893. These clinker-built, double-ended open rowing boats also carried a dipping lug sail of up to 120 square feet. The hull was shaped to allow the boat to ride through the breakers to the shore – the crew then used the oars protruding from orruck holes to carry the boat up the steep shingle beach. The group portrait was by the pioneering photography firm Frith & Co.

LEFT: Frank Hurley shoots a 'motion picture' from the jib boom of *Discovery,* as she heads south toward Antarctica, 1929.

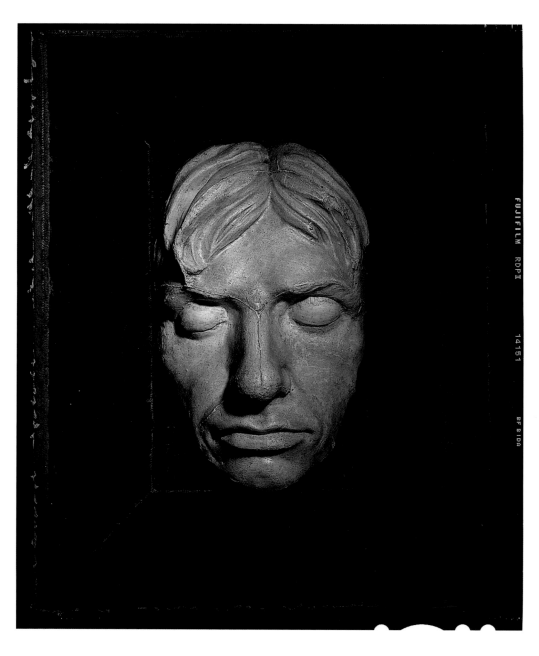

RIGHT: This rare cast of Admiral Nelson's face was for many years believed to be a death mask, made after the Battle of Trafalgar in 1805. It was bought by Queen Mary in 1924 from an antique shop in the Isle of Wight and is now in the collections of the Royal Naval Museum in Portsmouth. Recent research suggests that this cast was actually created when the naval hero was alive, though admittedly rather unwell, travelling through Vienna in 1800. It is, perhaps, as near to Nelson's true appearance as we are ever likely to find.

waves. The negative cast was cleaned and then filled with plaster to provide a positive – the mask we see here. Features were refined. Sometimes the eyes were opened, as if the subject has been captured in a moment of action, a little like the modern celebrity caught unawares by the flash of a camera. Nelson's mask was used as the *modello* for a number of marble busts. Countless copies were made, legitimately and otherwise. These sculptures gave many artists an impression of the man they would,

in turn, make the star of their grand oil canvases. Prints from these pictures were runaway successes and the cheap engravings that began to circulate as soon as he stepped ashore in England made Nelson 'one of the most recognisable faces in Britain'.

In just five years, however, Nelson would be dead. Mortally wounded in one of the most ferocious sea battles the world had ever seen, this ocean hero never lived to have his photograph taken. It is fitting he begins our story though as we join him at the dawn of a new century. Old forms of image making were soon to be engulfed by the new. The Battle of Trafalgar, his defining moment, also marks the decisive turning point for the rest of this maritime century. It is no overstatement to say that his victory, that fateful October day in 1805, shaped the future of nations across the globe. With supremacy of the seas secured, Britain took to the oceans as never before. Through an energetic century of overseas trade and travel, technological innovation and commercial opportunity, the face of the world was changed forever.

Yet for Nelson the passage of time was unkind. Though his status as England's greatest modern hero was consecrated in that bittersweet triumph at sea, in recent years historians have looked to excavate the man from the myth, to lift the mask and discover his true character. For a great many people he is a scandalous figure, an 'arrogant philanderer', the wager of war. For others, he means nothing at all – a hero long forgotten, irrelevant to the modern world, shamed by our neglect. Though Nelson's statue looms high above London's Trafalgar Square, it is often hard to see past the legend, past an image of the hero that history has passed down. We have no photographs to help us. This rare mask is the most authentic image we have of Nelson, certainly more *truthful* than the endless portraits that were painted of him, but is this enough? Imagine for a moment if he had survived into the age of photography, like many of those who served alongside him. If only a daring cameraman could have been at his side that tempestuous day off the Spanish coast. What else could photographs tell us about the rise, and fall, of this enigmatic man?

A DROP IN THE OCEAN

The history of human encounter with the sea, and of the sociology, poetry and politics of the oceans, could comprise, it has been said, a 'history of man'. Journeying upon the sea is one of our greatest adventures. This present book is a celebration of maritime achievement told through some of the world's best marine photographs. However, the ocean is vast and its story, much, much larger. Through migration, commerce, industry, war-making and science, tourism and enterprise, photographs of the ocean have been generated on a great scale, but photography coincides with just a brief moment in the long history of our relationship with the sea. This book may be thought of as a simple sketch, a short note for an essay that might contribute to a huge

library of ocean activity. The challenge has been to draw out images with interesting stories and historical significance, while well aware that a single photograph is, for want of a better analogy, just a 'drop in the ocean'. We have selected some 235 images in all from archives and professional collections totalling well over a million images. Our central portfolio has just 100 portraits – less than the number of images in the free newspaper you might read on the train.

This *maritime album* is then, by necessity, but a glimpse of the long history of ambition and adventure on the seas. One hopes there is something here to satisfy the casual reader and the most ardent of nautical experts. There should be much in between for the enthusiast. And that is, in a way, what this book aims to achieve – to serve as an accessible introduction to

The photograph, as keepsake, as legacy, as a window on the past, retains huge power.

some famous 'faces', while also bringing forward some characters whose lives deserve to be more widely known. I am mindful of the way one edits and ignores: images that are now pushed to the margins might be the star attraction in a different context. This is neither a definitive account of marine photography, nor a complete history of the photographic portrait. I am not sure such a thing is wanted, or even possible.

It was our intention to include all manner of people who voyaged across the oceans or who have been inspired by the sea to do great things. Men, like Nelson, who fell doing their duty, who died doing what they loved. Men who were lost at sea before they could return to loved ones. Photographs are cherished and emotive objects. Sometimes, only one tantalizing image of a person survives, often none at all. The photograph, as keepsake, as legacy, as a window on the past, retains huge power. Frequently images are so evocative they have become shorthand for a person, a symbol of everything they may have done in life. Courageous women are also featured here. It has been difficult to find photographs of sea-faring ladies in photography's early years, but now women fight alongside their male colleagues in the world's navies, they set records in yacht-racing leaving others in their wake, they row the Atlantic or explore the ocean's depths while their husbands look after the children at home. Much, thankfully, has changed since Nelson's day.

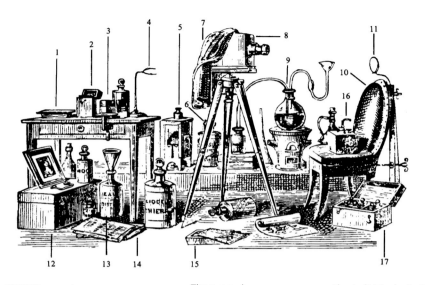

ABOVE: 'Daguerreotype apparatus suitable for a portrait', an illustration from a French photography manual, 1850. The essential kit is as follows: 1. buffing block; 2. plate storage box; 3. plate vice; 4. plate rest for gilding; 5. mercury chamber with alcohol burner at top; 6. fixing solution; 7. darkcloth for focussing; 8. half-plate camera; 9. retort for distilled water; 10. posing chair; 11. head rest; 12. equipment carry case; 13. distilled water; 14. technical manuals; 15. plateholder and plate; 16. quarter-plate smaller camera on chair; 17. chemicals box.

RIGHT: A gallery of unknown mariners, sixth-plate (8x7 cm) daguerreotypes, 1848-55. These small portraits were treasured keepsakes for families separated by the sea-faring life. Though neither a ship nor the ocean appears in the image, they are quintessential examples of maritime photography. A guide from the 1850s would suggest: 'Who can be without a daguerreotype of him or her they love? That embodiment – as it were, of the form's spirit – that exquisite and perfect impress of the features? Yes, it does raise the mind from earth to heaven, and bring to the imagination the spiritual forms of the dear departed, and makes us hope and wish to join them in eternity'.

There are, however, many worthy individuals that have been left out, many whose achievements alone merit their inclusion. Space forces my hand. Often when researching, each turn of the page brings forward yet another person about whom you would love to know more. It's perhaps not enough to justify the mix of people here as those whose stories have most interested me, but it remains, unashamedly, a main element of my selection. Frequently, those people I was lucky to meet in making this book suggested their historical favourites, even introducing me to the people who they themselves have been inspired by. It is a pleasure to be able to include some of these figures here.

Some may complain that there is too much attention paid to naval types – a crew of 'be-whiskered or be-medalled Admirals', best forgotten. That would be ungenerous, but I would admit this is where my interests often lie. Already too much Nelson? Quite possibly. Back to 1800 for a moment and even Nelson was unsure that he deserved to be remembered. He was so worn out, he wrote, that he felt but a shadow of himself remained. He was consumed with self-doubt and even his beloved career was in jeopardy: 'who wants a one-eyed, one-armed admiral? My life is finished'. Though Nelson drew crowds of admirers, for many he remained a disappointment, his reputation over-hyped and his appearance unremarkable. In Germany, one observer would declare: 'Nelson is one of the most insignificant figures I ever saw ... a more miserable collection of bones and wizened frame cannot be imagined. He speaks little, and then only in English, and he hardly ever smiles'. It is clear, whatever you do, you can never please everyone.

THE TIDE OF CHANGE

Photographs are now so familiar they have almost become invisible. Our world is dominated by images; we look at them endlessly, we carry them around, they represent us and provide our identities, they both reveal and obscure. Photographs speed around the globe, jumping from our phones to our computers, inhabiting a digital space that is rarely material and infrequently real. As we walk down a city street, or drive our cars, or travel overseas, we are being automatically photographed by a fleet of cameras, often not directly operated by humans at all. It's hard to imagine a world free of the photograph and there is no turning back now. The brash and vibrant visual culture of the photograph is permanent and omnipresent. What may seem more remarkable though, is that it all began in an attic workroom, deep in the French countryside. The year was 1826.

The French inventor Joseph Nicéphore Niépce is now rightly considered the first to fix a photographic image. His 'heliograph' view out of his window had taken almost eight hours of 'sun drawing' to expose on a polished pewter plate. He later teamed up with another flamboyant Frenchman, the Parisian dioramist Louis-Jacques-Mandé Daguerre, to develop the technique. Daguerre outlived his ally and went on to declare his technological breakthroughs to the world in 1839. His silvered copper plates, when revealed to sunlight, were able to produce images of intricate detail and accuracy. One of the earliest of these 'daguerreotypes', made in 1837, was an image of his studio, a corner littered with plaster casts and marble busts; those old forms of portraiture rendered obsolete. *La Gazette de France* declared the new invention to be so significant as to 'upset all scientific theories on light and optics' and thus 'revolutionise the art of drawing'. The American writer Edgar Allan Poe was equally enchanted, calling it 'the most important, and perhaps the most extraordinary triumph of modern science'. When the secrets were divulged at a sitting of the French Academy of Sciences, a mob stormed the building. The artist Paul Delaroche gasped that 'from this day, painting is dead'.

In the 1840s, once it had become commercially viable, the daguerreotype surpassed the oil painting, the plaster cast, the miniature and silhouette to become the most popular form of portraiture. Nonetheless, it was still a long and complicated process. A copper plate was electroplated with silver and buffed to a mirror-like finish. The plate was exposed to iodine fumes forming the photosensitive silver iodide on the plate's surface.

It was then placed into a light-tight plate holder in the darkroom until it was ready to be loaded into the back of a camera. The cover was then pulled from the front of the plate holder and the lens cap removed, exposing the plate to the light reflected off the sitter, who was often clamped to a chair to eliminate movement that would blur the image. It's partly because of this that we have a view of early Victorians as rigid and stiff – the portraits they so desired demanded it. By 1853 it is estimated that in New York City there were some eighty-six portrait galleries, almost half of them on Broadway alone.

A visit to one of these studios was a fashionable recreation. In Boston, for example, America's elite flocked to the studio of Southworth and Hawes. Famous faces photographed for the first time there included entrepreneur George Peabody, abolitionist Cassius Marcellus Clay, champion of the poor Richard Henry Dana Jnr and luminous authors such as Oliver Wendell Holmes, Harriet Beecher Stowe, Longfellow and Emerson. Anxious to join them was Donald McKay, a man on the rise as the builder of some of the finest ships in the world. His first, the *Stag Hound*, launched in 1850, was followed by many others including the behemoth *Great Republic* and the clipper *Flying Cloud*, which sped across the oceans during the California Gold Rush. At its launch in 1854, McKay's clipper *Champion of the Seas* became the largest sailing vessel in the world and the one of the fastest. In a period of 24 hours that December, she sailed some 465 nautical miles, a record which stood for over a century. McKay's modern portrait was then a statement of his success: a man making good in this brave new world. He liked it so much he had replicas displayed in the cabins of his vessels. He also engaged Southworth to capture a number of views of his prolific shipyard – a rare, haunting image survives, perhaps the earliest photograph of this maritime industry.

But despite its initial popularity, particularly in France and the United States, the daguerreotype suffered from a series of basic disadvantages that soon led to it being overtaken by other means of photographic recording. It's often described as photography's 'false start'. Exposure times were just too long and though this was eventually reduced to minutes rather than hours, it still placed limitations on the choice of subject, rendering the energetic world into which it had been born static and immobile. The delicate surface of the daguerreotype was easily scratched and so was covered by glass and enclosed in small leather cases, framed in gold, wrapped in velvet.

It would be William Henry Fox Talbot who produced the first positive-negative photographic process, thus allowing multiple copies to be made from a single image. It was a technique that was destined to become the basis of modern photography and it ensured the medium the reach and prevalence to make it a genuine mass cultural product. Talbot had begun experimenting while on his honeymoon in Italy in 1833, but had kept his research a secret. Daguerre's announcement drew

This was a bold and energetic age and the pace of innovation was all-consuming.

him to reveal his own and by 1840 he printed his first 'Talbotype' – or *calotype*, meaning the beautiful picture – and after gradual improvement it would eclipse Daguerre's process. He used sensitised paper as his base and produced, in the camera, a negative image that was later placed in a printing frame with a new sheet of sensitised paper behind it. After exposure, a print was produced by contact by the action of light alone and then fixed in common salt.

The innovative process enabled illustration in *The Pencil of Nature*, which Talbot started to publish in 1844. Not only was it the first book to contain photographic images, it also provided, in a sense, a visual language for a new generation of practitioners. It was both an advertisement for the art and its manifesto – a call to arms. Soon, photographs would be seen everywhere, from bookshelves to street corners. The previous year, the young engineer Isambard Brunel had presented to the world his 332-foot *Great Britain*, often considered the first modern ship. She was built of iron rather than wood, powered by an engine rather than with the wind, and became the first propellor-driven ship to cross the Atlantic. This was a bold and energetic age and the pace of innovation was all-consuming.

Though photography describes only a 'thin chronological slice of the story of man and the sea', that slice represents a rich period of social and technological change. When photography was first announced to the world in 1839, the majority of the world's population was still unknown to the West. The oceans were more unfamiliar still. And yet, within a hundred years, this new pictorial system would make possible huge advances in human understanding, from the seafloor to the surface of the moon. The development of the photographic art is a hymn to our desire to glimpse the unseen, to reach for the unknown. But, all that was yet to come. In the early years, the new 'camera artists' were trying simply

LEFT: The various small studio cabinet cards and the still smaller *carte-de-visite* were ideally suited to the needs of mariners and their families. As generations of Victorians embarked on long voyages, portraits of wives and children travelled the world in their husband's breast pockets. At foreign ports – like Malta, Sydney, Hong Kong and Zanzibar – a portrait became a memento to send home with a letter. From top left to bottom right: A young boy, by C. Bräunlich of Rudolstadt, 1901; veteran mariner George Read with his various campaigns medals, 1885; Lieutenant William Brown, HMS *Penelope*, 1856; Captain John 'White Hat' Willis of the tea clipper *Cutty Sark*, 1875; Young children in a pasteboard boat, by C. Klee of Schönebeck, 1910; Seaman Scott, 'Remember Me', carte by Young Seng, 'Marine Ship and Portrait Painter', Hong Kong, 1920; Unidentified sailor, J. Mallia's Grand Studio, Malta, 1900; Vice-Admiral Sir Cyprian Bridge, commanding officer of the China Station, with officers of HMS *Agincourt*, Hong Kong, 1903.

ABOVE: The American inventor George Eastman introduced his Kodak camera to the world in 1888. Small and light enough to be held in the hands, it was sold already loaded with film to take one hundred photographs. After the film had been exposed, the entire camera was returned to the factory for the film to be developed and printed. The camera, reloaded with fresh film, was then returned to its owner together with a set of circular snapshot prints, two and a half inches in diameter. From top to bottom: George Eastman poses with his Kodak camera, on board *Gallia* crossing the Atlantic, 1890; Children paddling in the sea, 1895; A beach photographer stands by his mobile studio, 1895.

to describe life on their own streets. They would soon venture further afield, to where the land meets the sea. It would not be long before they stepped away from the shore altogether.

Though it would be a mistake to read the history of the photograph as a series of perpetual, overtaking breakthroughs, it is right to note the major changes that were celebrated at the time. By 1851, for example, Frederick Scott Archer, an English sculptor, produced what was known as the wet *collodion* process, in which negatives were made from a solution of guncotton dissolved in ether and applied to glass plates. It superseded Talbot's calotype but had the major drawback that developing had to take place immediately after the image was captured. The ambrotype made its appearance in 1851 as a cheaper alternative to the daguerreotype and it lasted well into the 1860s. The silver plate was swapped for a glass plate coated in sensitised collodion. This too was replaced in 1856 by the ferrotype or tintype, with a thin sheet-iron plate instead of the ambrotype's fragile glass. With the advent of glass plates, retouching was possible and, unsurprisingly, almost everyone wanted their portraits 'beautified' in this way – although they may not have liked to admit it. 'When it comes to retouching', the author of *Naturalistic Photography* would declare, 'straightening noses and removing double chins, flattening cheeks and smoothing skins, we thus descend to an abyss of charlatanism and jugglery'. By 1870, the wet plate, in turn, was made obsolete and by 1877 an English physician Richard Maddox introduced the *gelatin dry plate*. An age of instantaneous photography was at hand.

Cameras would also change rapidly. The hand-crafted wooden and brass boxes with fixed lenses used by Talbot were handsome affairs – essentially *objets d'art* rather than technical tools – but they were soon improved, reduced in size and cost, and became more widely available. Petzval, a Viennese mathematician, and Voigtländer, an optician, worked on improving lenses and revealed their orthoscopic 'correct seeing' lens in 1857. Others experimented with glass negatives coated with albumen – egg white – which rendered details scrupulously. Albumen paper was introduced by Blanquart-Évrard in 1850 and would be widely used throughout the rest of the century. At its peak, the Dresdner Albumin Papier Fabrik, the largest manufacturer in Europe, used 60,000 fresh eggs a day. Photographers also set about organising themselves – in 1851 the Société Héliographique was formed in Paris and in 1853 the Photographic Society in London – and many were able to make a profession of the new technology.

The following year, the French photographer André Disdéri exploited the demand by inventing a camera that took eight photographs on a single glass plate. The result was the *carte-de-visite*, the in-vogue calling card. As Julie Bonaparte wrote in her diary in 1856: 'It is the fashion to have your portrait made small in a hundred copies – it only costs fifty francs and it is very handy to give to your friends and to have their images constantly at hand'. Napoleon III duly placed an order for hundreds of cards printed with his portrait. Pictures supplemented names and identity became a matter of images rather than words. In London, Mayall and Co made sets of portraits of Queen Victoria *en famille* which sold in their hundreds of thousands at a guinea a dozen. The cheap *carte* proved so popular that the lower classes began to have their portraits taken too, pasting them into albums, sharing them with their loved ones. Small children perch in mock rowing-boats or among the rigging of a pasteboard pirate galleon. Pretty girls with fresh curls parade in their favourite frocks, jaunty sailors puff out their chests, young blades in tall hats lean against cases full of books they will never read. Make-believe, memorial, fun and fancy combined; the photographic image was growing up fast.

By 1884 the first flexible negative film was produced, necessitating another dramatic change in equipment. A few years later George Eastman presented the first Kodak camera, a name he chose because it 'could be pronounced anywhere in the world'. It was small, with a single speed of 1/25 second and a fixed focus, but it was revolutionary in two simple ways: relatively cheap and easy to use. It was a snapshot camera for the masses, with the now famous slogan: 'You press the button, we do the rest'. With the arrival of the Browine at the turn of the century, the camera was offered for sale at five shillings (or one dollar). Photography was democratised, open to everyone. It had become the most mobile and accessible of all visual forms. 'Now every *nipper* has a *Brownie*', the photographer Alvin Coburn despaired, 'a photograph is as common as a box of matches'. The enthusiastic amateur photographer and professional cynic George Bernard Shaw, observed 'the photographer is like a cod which lays a million eggs in order that one may be hatched'. From that point on, photographs and cameras could, literally, be carried anywhere in the pocket. For a trip to the seaside, a short holiday overseas, or a long voyage to exotic lands, the Kodak was ready to capture it all.

BESIDE THE SEASIDE

We join the pioneering Scottish photographers, David Octavius Hill and Robert Adamson, walking along the rocky beach near Newhaven. It's a summer's day in 1844. With Fox Talbot's techniques to guide them, they have travelled just north of Edinburgh in search of curious fisherfolk and beautiful sailboats. They had met the previous year when Adamson was tasked with creating reference photographs for Hill's vast massed portrait painting of a turbulent meeting of Church of Scotland ministers. Adamson created the calotypes, Hill as the artist supplied the direction. Finding the clerics a rather uninteresting lot, they began making portraits of well-to-do Edinburgh notables, but their finest work would come when venturing among the working-class communities on the coast of the Forth estuary.

Sailors appear in broad-brimmed hats and tarry trousers, fisher-girls with their baskets and striped petticoats bring in the oysters and herring and help mend the nets. These are not only some of the very first maritime portraits, but they also mark photography's first appearance as a tool of social enquiry. The duo were photographing subjects to celebrate what they saw as proof of the *virtues* of the maritime life. The periodic slumps of the Industrial Revolution, the Highland clearances, the pall of famine and disease, had driven the poor into the cities and generated chaotic slums.

Though work in Newhaven was hard and hazardous, the fisherfolk there were flourishing through 'pious toil'. Though at times candid, at times contrived, Hill and Adamson's marine portraits are, nonetheless, innovative. They were the first to make photography a documentary field, creating portraits with a purpose – giving photography a life. They would work together for four years, until abruptly, Adamson died. Hill turned his attention back to the task of painting his huge crowd canvas. It was meant to be finished in 1846 but took almost twenty-one years to complete. Photography however, was moving fast.

Freed from the confines of the studio, amateurs and artists alike stationed their instruments in front of abbeys, castles, beauty spots, harbours and beaches. Look into the albums of John Dillwyn Llewelyn, a distinguished photographer and relative of Fox Talbot, and one catches a glimpse of upper-class family life by the sea: social excursions, boating, escapades among rock-pools and craggy caves. In the summer of 1854, armed with his camera, Llewelyn set out to 'attack the restless waves' of Caswell Bay and he would be awarded a silver medal at the Exposition Universelle in Paris for his efforts. His photographs, entitled 'Motion', were shown in London too, attracting some attention:

> Mr Llewelyn ... has sent four instantaneous pictures, in one of which the seashore has been taken, with

ABOVE: As much as the Kodak technology was innovative, so too were its advertising campaigns. The introduction of portable cameras encouraged more women to take photographs and Kodak recognised their potential as a major new market. By 1912 the 'Kodak Girl', with her famous striped dress, had become the central theme of their advertising and would be featured in posters across four decades. She also appeared on top of this remarkable travelling photographic float, which parked on seaside promenades to enhance sales amongst holidaymakers. A poster on the side of the lorry reads: 'Save your happy memories with a Kodak'.

carts and persons moving upon it. Waves are caught with foam on them, and fixed while they are rolling; and the faintest trace of indecision in some walking figures shows that they could scarcely have completed one footstep before the picture was complete. Another represents a steamboat at a pier, and has fixed instantaneously the floating smoke and steam.

Thrilling, sublime, threatening, serene: the oceans continue to be a huge source of artistic inspiration and it is no surprise that the photographic medium naturally followed man's innate attraction to the sea. Though the slowness of early processes confined some photographers to static motifs – small fishing craft wallowing in mudflats, or the giant new steamships ready to race from their jetties – some began to experiment with moving craft. By 1851, the Le Havre photographers Warnod and Macaire were able to daguerreotype vessels moving in and out of port. As a young man, Francis J. Mortimer would spend three years on the Scilly Isles recording the huge winter seas by venturing out in pilot gigs. He clambered over rocky headlands with a self-styled waterproof camera, a rope tied round his waist and a band of helpers lest he be swept from the shore.

The other major challenge for marine photography concerned levels of light. Ever since Fox Talbot had experimented with images of the seashore at Swansea many were intrigued by the photographic complexities of the sea – balancing shifting skies, reflections off the water, while maintaining an exposure brief enough to retain the shapes of waves and surf. Yet, wet-collodion negatives were extremely sensitive to blue light. In simple terms, this meant that if a photographer making a landscape had exposed the land correctly, the sky would be overexposed and come out as a bald, white blank in the print. Overcoming this problem, photographers learnt to make two negatives, one exposed to capture detail in the sky, one the land, or in some cases, the sea. When the two negatives were then printed together, in theory, a correctly balanced landscape would be created. Charles Breese's instantaneous sea and cloud studies, complete with imitation moonlight, drew crowds to the stands at the International Exhibition in 1862. 'Every drop of water in the waves dashing and breaking against the rock and tumbling headlong into the foaming cataract; the seagulls skimming across the wave, the ocean lashed into turbulence by the tempest, rare sunset and moonlit views, are amongst his triumphs', rejoiced a reviewer.

French photographic genius Gustave Le Gray was the first to master this combination printing technique, creating some of the most admired photographs of the 1850s. He spent the summer of 1856 capturing the coastal shipping of Normandy and the pictures were expansive enough to give some idea of what it might be like to navigate on the ocean, with its range of winds and tides. His *Brig upon the Water* was the first photographic seascape to become truly famous as a work of art, with an interplay of clouds, sea and sunlight that anticipated the later Impressionists. On technical grounds alone it was pioneering, since most photographs of that decade rarely attempted to capture a ship moving freely at sea. Fortified by the positive public response, he took his camera to the Mediterranean coast in 1857, travelling by a newly opened railroad to Sète. At the French Photographic Society exhibition, held in Paris later that year, Le Gray's 'astonishing seacapes' were given top ranking. 'We are not in the least surprised', ran one review, 'that these enchanted scenes are all the rage'. The following summer he was invited to Cherbourg to photograph the peacetime meeting of the French and British Fleets, capturing newsworthy images of ships at sea, flags flying and cannon salvos firing. Nelson would have been amazed how much the world had changed in just fifty years. Yet, truth be told, within a decade Le Gray's photographic business would fail. He left debts, a wife and children behind and fled to the Middle East to become a drawing teacher in Cairo. He died there in 1884 never having returned home.

The habit of city-dwellers visiting the coast had begun on the advice of eighteenth-century doctors, who prescribed the benefits of a brisk walk and a lung-full of fresh sea air for their wealthy patients. It was not until the coming of the railways in the 1840s, higher wages and the rise of leisure time, that the habits of the gentility could be adopted by the mass public. Within just fifty years the coast was changed forever – with cheap lodgings, steamer excursions, pleasure boats and pier-end variety shows all meeting the needs of the new summer tourist. The seaside would become part of every child's life. Charles Dodgson, a keen portrait photographer himself, would write in *Alice's Adventures in Wonderland* that 'wherever you go to on the English coast you find a number of bathing machines in the sea, some children digging in the sand with wooden spades, then a row of lodging houses and behind them a railway station'. Some *sea-siders* would lounge with a good book in a deckchair. Others might relax by aiming their telescopes out to sea, and toward the herd of bathing machines, perhaps catching a tasty glimpse of those taking a plunge. 'Most bathers are all severely inspected', one writer announced, 'not only as they confusedly ascend from the sea, but as they kick and sprawl and flounder about in its muddy margins, like mermaids in flannel smocks'. Donkey rides and sandcastles, other paddlers with trousers rolled to the knee, faces covered with ice-cream and big smiles; the beach provided photographs that became synonymous with the fun and freedom of the ocean.

The resorts attracted a new generation of photographers who were quick to set up business and take advantage of the visitors at play. It was at the seaside – whether the beach, pier or promenade – that many people experienced their first photograph; a holiday token, an amusement to share with friends when they returned home, sunburnt and well-spent. In 1870, the first American beachside boardwalk was built in Atlantic City and tintype photographers flocked to the scene. An English tourist vividly described his visit there, at the seaside studio of Harry Smith:

> As for me I go and get photographed. A couple of bathers in blue jerseys and short drawers come out as I go in, for Harry Smith announces he makes a specialty of swimmers. He has two attitudes for them; one shading the eyes and looking off right, in the stage-sailor fashion; the other sitting in a section of boat, a life-belt around the neck, an oar in the hand. For me, a walking gentleman, he brings forth a rickety piece of balustrade, an imitation India-rubber plant, and a background of a lighthouse and a sea-gull ... 'Not so bad, eh?' he says affably, handing me eight versions of myself alternately very black and very white, like underdone or badly-burnt toast. Then he offers me a large collodion-stained fist to shake, and turns briskly to the lady bathers who are arranging their long thin locks coquettishly before the studio glass.

The finest of these photographers was certainly Francis Frith – a wholesale grocer turned wealthy traveller – who used his business acumen to dominate the new market. Returning from grand excursions through Egypt and Palestine, in 1860 he set out with the intention of photographing every city, town and village in Britain. For the next thirty years he crossed the country by train and pony-and-trap, producing

ABOVE LEFT: A great fleet of herring drifters gather at Scarborough as bathing machines jostle on the shoreline, September 1897. The turn of the century was to see a rapid growth in steam-powered fishing and within just a decade fleets like this were consigned to history. Scarborough was Britain's first seaside resort and it was tourism that would become the main focus of activity in the town.

ABOVE: Comic postcards by Tom Browne, showing the 'pleasures' of a cruise, an old-fashioned beach photographer with the Spudds family, and the cheeky amateur snapshot photographer about to get his comeuppance, 1910.

images of beauty spots and summer attractions that were bought by millions of Victorian tourists. Soon his studio was supplying shops nationwide and he gathered about him a team of photographers to meet the demand. From holiday portraits to the new picture postcards, the seaside was a photographer's dream. By 1890, with some 2,000 outlets to his name, Frith had created the greatest specialist photographic publishing company in the world.

Other enterprising photographers took their cameras to foreign shores. When Roger Fenton photographed the Crimean War, for example, he travelled with thirty-six large chests of paraphernalia, bellows-cameras, trunks of plate glass, chests of chemicals, rubber baths, printing frames, stoves and tinned food, all stowed in his 'Photographic Van' – a wine-merchant's wagon fitted out as a mobile darkroom. Though Fenton is most remembered for his portraits of doomed cavalry officers and vast battlefields strewn with cannonballs, his photographs of ordnance wharves, the tangle of transport ships and stevedores, munitions and mortar batteries, brought the grim realities of this disorganised war before a domestic audience. Though still confined to the edges of the sea, this was maritime photography's first foray into a theatre of conflict. In the twentieth century some of the most dramatic and challenging ocean imagery would come from actions in the North Atlantic and hostile engagements in the Pacific. It was Fenton who first aimed the camera at the ships of war.

Others would direct their attention beneath the waves. There is no space here to detail the long history of ocean studies, but one name stands out, Sir John Murray. From his first major voyage, as ship's surgeon on an Arctic whaling expedition in 1868 to his last research cruise on *Michael Sars* in the North Atlantic in 1910, he would fundamentally change the way people thought about the sea. He was an assistant on the four-year expedition to explore the deep oceans of the globe on *Challenger*, travelling nearly 70,000 nautical miles. Murray would edit and publish over fifty volumes of reports about the voyage. He is often credited as the founding father of modern oceanography – he was, indeed, the first to use the term – being the first to discover the Mid-Atlantic Ridge and oceanic trenches. He improved methods of collecting plankton, he mapped sea-floor deposits and ocean currents and perfected the measuring of temperatures and salinity at depth. At every step photography made itself useful in recording the techniques required. Interestingly, it is possible that some of the very earliest photographic kit –

both daguerreotype apparatus and sensitised paper for Talbot's photogenic drawings – travelled on James Clark Ross' voyage to Antarctica in 1839-43, an expedition, it was said, that was 'admirably equipped and every way furnished with instruments of Science and Art'. Shortly before the ships *Erebus* and *Terror* departed for the South, surgeon Robert McCormick wrote that he was hopeful of 'obtaining faithful representations of those evanescent forms inhabiting the ocean'. Sadly, no photographic images from this voyage survive. A comment from another member of the expedition, suggests why this was the case: '... we left England provided with a register for every known phenomena of nature though certainly not qualified to cope with them all'.

As the years passed though, other adventurous photographers met with considerable success. I admire, for example, the Scottish geographer John Thomson, who journeyed among Sumatran jungles and the ruined cities of Cambodia and would later spend almost five years travelling through China with his camera. He was initially in business manufacturing marine chronometers and nautical instruments and set up a photo studio in Singapore, taking portraits of wealthy European merchants enriching themselves on the Eastern trade. Though little known today, Thomson became one of the leading champions of photography; writing articles, creating portraits for the Royal Family, instructing fellows of the Royal Geographical Society and editing Tissandier's *History and Handbook of Photography*, which became a standard reference work. 'Photography is a power placed in our hands', he described:

... it is a novel experiment to attempt to illustrate a book of travels with photographs, a few years back so perishable, and so difficult to reproduce ... we are now making history, and the sun picture supplies the means of passing down a record of what we are, and what we have achieved in this nineteenth century of progress.

For his next adventure, Thomson explored London's darkest corners – showing a world as unfamiliar to his middle-class audience as the exotic Far East. The result was *Street Life in London*, published in eleven parts from 1876, with stunning portraits of 'Cast Iron Billy, 'Hookey Alf', of swagmen and whelk-mongers, beggars and boot-blacks. In championing the urban poor and the dens of the dockside – impoverished, unique, dangerous – Thomson was pioneering a new type of investigative, visual study, marrying images with the printed word. Photojournalism was born.

Others, too numerous to mention, would follow in Thomson's wake. I think of Peter Emerson's tours through an archaic East Anglia, filled with reed-cutters and heavy-limbed labourers, boatmen and limpet-pickers, a land of mists, water lilies, broad sails and far horizons. This was an imagined Fen country, a rustic idyll, a photographic antidote to keep sprawling England at bay, to 'drown out the barrel-organs and beer saloons'. His images would have many successors; such as the Germany of ancient oaks and medieval towers in the troubled 1920s and a France awash with peasants and vineyards in the lens of Cartier-Bresson and André Kertész. Emerson's quest for the rural-maritime was paralleled in a way by Frank Sutcliffe, the renowned portrait photographer of Whitby, a whaling town nestled on the Yorkshire coast. His fascination was in genre of the kind practiced by the naturalist painters of Brittany and Cornwall – his cast were fishermen and their womenfolk, conversing on the quayside, arranging their catches, scouring the rock-pools for bait. Like Emerson, Sutcliffe was disturbed by the passing of old ways, a vanishing world. His town, once famous for boatbuilding and fishing, was relying more and more on the annual flood of tourists: 'garish sounds of hurdy-gurdies replaced the noise of the shipyards; sailing boats were replaced by steamers, and rowing boats by motor launches'. Sutcliffe's portraits were both a celebration and a lament. They were invitations to dream about the sea.

Yet Sutcliffe was also quick to embrace the new, becoming one of the first established photographers to be interested in snapshots. He was persuaded to try one of the lightweight and inexpensive cameras introduced in the 1890s and admitted that it was more convenient than anything he used before, perfect for 'these hectic times'. A friend who met him in 1900 said that Sutcliffe had four Kodaks slung about his body. His hand camera became the photographic equivalent of an artist's sketch-book, a kind of visual diary to record the world around him:

The Kodak has freshened my interest in outdoor photography in a marked degree, though my friends chaff me and ask if I sleep with 'that thing' under my pillow, and take it to church with me on Sundays. 'That thing' helps me remember what I might otherwise forget – the countless charms which nature puts on for the pleasure of all those who have eyes to see.

Lifeboat launchings, fisher-girls packing oak barrels, young boys swimming in the harbour – Sutcliffe's Kodak drank it all in. He would also take quayside snaps down in Cornwall, where both photographers and painters were creating an industry out of fishing images and, as in other places in Britain and abroad, helping to redefine whole regions for tourism.

Lightweight, or 'detective' cameras as they became known, made it possible for the photographer to be alert to unique moments of activity, to a world of movement and variety. The photographic genius Alfred Stieglitz, writing in 1897, scorned most of what had been achieved with these cameras, thinking them only 'good for the purposes of the globe-trotter, who wished to jot down photographic notes'. But hand cameras were inevitable and the 'jotters' captured life with prolific abandon. The Italian Count Giuseppe Primoli became famous for his spontaneous images of the idling nobility, street-vendors in Rome, sailors and sweethearts. In 1889 he had a plan to photograph the Shah of Persia on a night commode and he snapped Degas buttoning his trousers outside a public toilet. Spy cameras gradually appeared, in umbrellas, disguised in briefcases, coat buttons and suspenders. In England, Paul Martin trawled the coastal resorts with his Facile camera hidden in a wooden box wrapped in brown paper, stealing candid shots of paddlers at play and couples embracing on the sands. His images would appear in the new magazines which celebrated the sensational and the everyday. Photography was thus set on its modern course.

The high-spirited resort of Brighton was the *flâneur's* delight, its beaches and esplanades the perfect venue for a photographer of independent means like George Ruff Jnr. He prowled the promenade with his camera, snatching pictures of young ladies as they frolicked their way through the short English summer. At Hastings, George Wood's snapshots captured the leisured gaiety of the time – ranks of deckchairs and beach-huts and

ABOVE: A group of aspiring yachtsmen loiter round Cowes in the Isle of Wight. This engraving from *The Illustrated London News* in the summer of 1846 was drawn by Hablot Knight Browne, most famous as 'Phiz', the superlative illustrator of the novels of Charles Dickens.

LEFT: The steam trawler *Fuchsia* undergoing repairs at Milford Haven, 24 April 1909. In September 1916, she was captured by a German submarine while fishing in the North Sea. The crew were taken as prisoners – the fishing boat was sunk.

a swirl of seaside shows and exposed ankles. Some saw these early, mobile ocean portraits as a threat to decency. In 1893, the *Weekly Times* announced 'that several decent young men are forming themselves a Vigilance Association with the purpose of thrashing cads with cameras who go about at seaside places taking snapshots of ladies emerging from the deep ... we wish the new society stout cudgels and much success'.

But the snapshot camera proved unstoppable. Free of rituals and old inhibitions, it became loved among the emerging citizens of the mass society. Press hack James Jarché would pursue the quintessential – the ship-builder, the sailor, the salty trawlerman all fell to his lightweight (and silent) miniature Leica. Jarché was born to French immigrant parents among the docks of east London. His father was a professional photographer, who spent much of his time 'taking pictures for the police of corpses fished from the river or seamen discovered near the wharves with their throats cut'. Aged just seven, young James would assist him. As a man Jarché became one of the most successful of the new breed of photo-journalists. Today his work is often overlooked, but his images in the 1930s helped define the energy and blind optimism of the era. His subjects seem dizzying in their variety: inventors of jet-engines and vast ocean liners, chemical laboratories and new hospitals, fashion shows, political summits,

With a tunnel being constructed under the Thames, and new telegraph cables being laid on the seabed, life *under* the waves was emerging as a new fascination to the Victorians.

office-workers learning to type. Yet, his fisherfolk smile proudly with their catch while the industry was set to consume itself; his dockworkers celebrate the launching of a ship just as other yards close. Though the pictures were singular, the stories were broad. This was a photography of history unfolding.

GLASS PLATES AND WOODEN BOATS

In the early years, long exposure times, cumbersome equipment, and the frustratingly variable elements of sunlight, reflection, wind and water, were enough to chase all but the most intrepid photographers back into their studios. Most photographs of ships – also known as

'portraits' – taken before the 1880s show them stationary in side profile, wallowing at anchor or lying alongside in the docks. Commercial photographers specialising in ship portraiture were turning up in all the major ports in Europe, America and Asia. Their customers in these vast new harbour complexes were the owners, designers, insurers, passengers and proud members of the crew and the taste was not so much artistic as documentary. It was not always easy for a photographer to free a vessel of the dockside clutter and take a successful image with a clear horizon. One Mr Parry, 'marine photographist', described his experiences for the readers of the *American Annual of Photography*:

The picture of a ship with numerous others behind, with their forest of poles, spars, and rigging, looks confused and mixed up, producing a very unsatisfactory photograph, and one not at all likely to please. If you have the vessel moved a few feet into a more suitable position, you are treated as if you wanted the world moved, and are subjected to a large amount of abuse from self-important underlings.

Other photographers were more successful. Fox Talbot took some of the first images quayside, down at the Dublin docks in the 1840s. His 'steady friend', the wealthy parson Calvert Jones, aimed his innovative kit at the merchant schooners and smacks, square-riggers and paddle-tugs tethered in the mud at Swansea, waiting for the incoming tide. From storm-tossed coasts to crowded piers, George Washington Wilson of Aberdeen was catching on camera the varied business of maritime Britain. In 1857 he secured the first photographs of battleships afloat and, on the request of the Queen, the Navy made special arrangements to fire whole broadsides for his benefit. His photographs of the roar of smoke at the mouths of the guns prompted pride and astonishment among the public. Wilson responded modestly: 'These effects really can be caught by anyone, without any super-excellent lenses, but considerable watching and waiting is necessary before an effect turns up which is both capable and worthy of being taken, and one must be ready to do it at once, or presto! It is too late'.

In 1863, the hack Patrick Barry's *Dockyard Economy and Naval Power* was illustrated with thirty-one pictures of shipping and steelworks. It is perhaps the earliest maritime book with photographs. The rapid increases in ocean-going traffic, for trade and transport, naturally attracted photographic attention and as expertise grew, photographers became numerous. José Sánchez in

Valencia and Carlo Naya in Venice were creating views of harbour life that combined the painterly tradition with the presence of the new marine technology – wide bays dressed with sea-walls and lighthouses, the gentle waters of lagoons carved by new steam launches. Alice Austen of Staten Island recorded shipping in and out of New York for decades. The tug masters Orison Beaton and Hiram Hudson of Puget Sound took a mass of fine maritime photographs for their bosses. Wilhelm Hester also had a mixed practice there photographing shipyards and launch ceremonies, timber-mills and cargo wharves, crewmen posing on deck and captains and their wives relaxing in their saloons. Dramatic photographic seascapes by Eugène Colliau and Charles Grassin, of ships leaving port with sails catching the wind, could go some way in meeting the dreams of those longing for the thrill of the high seas.

With a tunnel being constructed under the Thames, and new telegraph cables being laid on the seabed, life *under* the waves was emerging as a new fascination to the Victorians. The increasing public interest in undersea curiosities was satisfied in new aquariums, sensational amusement halls, earnest lectures and magic lantern shows. At Leicester Square's 'Royal Panopticon of Science and Art', with its photography studio on the roof, visitors could marvel at automatic sewing machines, a device for recording piano music, a giant concert organ and a luminous fountain shooting water into the air. But the star attraction was its polygonal glass tank, twenty-foot deep, in which swimmers and a plucky diver frolicked for the crowds. Not far away, at the Regent Street 'Polytechnic Institution', a diver loaded with weights walked about on the bottom of his tank, picking up coins tossed in by spectators. A visitor in 1841 described the scene:

> A diver, clothed in a patent water and air tight diving dress, goes down a ladder to the bottom of the reservoir of water, being supplied from the air pump with air through a tube that enters into his dress; he is when prepared to descend, the oddest looking creature ever seen, he has an immense helmet of white metal over his head, and in front of his eyes are two large thick pieces of glass protected by bars of metal. This helmet is strongly strapped to his water proof dress, and he then presents a most laughable appearance.

Even better, perhaps, was the three-ton cast-iron diving bell suspended from a crane, in which eager punters paid a shilling each to be lowered down into the water. Most were intrigued to see what 'underwater' looked like – while eager young chaps went down to 'enhance their standing in the bright eyes of the pretty girls' who looked on from the galleries above. Prince Albert himself took the plunge in 1840.

The first underwater photograph was by William Thompson in 1856, using a housed plate-camera attached to a rope. Setting up a small tent on the beach as his darkroom, he rowed out into Weymouth Bay to lower his camera on its iron tripod gently to the seabed. He operated the shutter by pulling a string from his boat. The exposure time was more than ten minutes and, despite the camera flooding, after a few attempts the faint outline of seaweed could be seen. In 1893, French zoologist Louis Boutan modified a detective camera within a monstrous water-tight copper box, and plunged into the waters of the Mediterranean in a full diving suit. He made further experiments with battery-powered underwater arc lights, but the results were poor and few were interested enough to follow him.

By 1913, John Ernest Williamson's illuminated photographs of the depths of Chesapeake Bay inspired him to attempt motion pictures. He made the first ever underwater film in the clear seas off the Bahamas, using an underwater observation chamber, which he called 'the photosphere'. Underwater colour photography was born with a shot of a hogfish, photographed off the Florida Keys in the Gulf of Mexico in 1926. The pioneers William Longley and *National Geographic* staff photographer Charles Martin had equipped themselves with waterproof cameras and highly-explosive magnesium flash powder for underwater illumination. But it would not be until much later, in the 1950s, that underwater photography really came of age. Photographer Luis Marden accompanied the legendary ocean explorer Jacques Cousteau on a voyage from Toulon to the Suez Canal aboard Cousteau's ship, *Calypso*. By journey's end, Marden had 1,200 photographs, the largest collection of underwater colour photographs yet taken.

Back in Portsmouth, the home of the Royal Navy, Alfred West would pioneer marine photography and movie-making in the crowded waters of the Solent. The resourceful son of a carpenter, he invented his own shutter release mechanism and a stabilising device, which enabled him to get right out on the water. His portrait of *Mohawk* racing at the Royal Southampton Yacht Club regatta in 1884 was awarded the gold medal of the St Louis Convention in America. Such was his success he could afford to take up the new and expensive art of cinematography and

TOP: 'Undersea explorers' at the Royal Naval Exhibition, 1891.

ABOVE: On 1 June 1939 the pride of the Royal Navy, His Majesty's Submarine *Thetis*, sank in Liverpool Bay during her sea trials. A major salvage operation was launched to save the lives of the crew trapped inside, just thirty-eight miles from land. Diver Lawson Smith attempted to reach the stricken submarine and take underwater images that might be of use to guide the rescue effort. A Leica camera was tied inside his helmet so that the trigger came between his teeth and the film could be wound on using his lips, but the rushing tide hampered his attempts. Another salvage diver died from the bends, rushing to the surface too quickly, after his guide rope came loose. The ninety-nine men on board were eventually overtaken by carbon dioxide poisoning, waiting for a rescue that never came.

created some of the first maritime footage – of a mine explosion and a torpedo being tested in the harbour. In 1898, he shipped aboard HMS *Crescent* to film and photograph events on the Royal cruise. He exhibited these films to the crew and then at Osborne House to Queen Victoria who was reported as being 'greatly pleased'. These films formed the basis of his first and very popular shows of maritime images that later toured the country. West described the scene:

> The stage was profusely decorated, the screen being draped with the Union Jack and the White Ensign flanked by palms and banks of flowers. A large orchestra was engaged together with a professional lady singer. The Hall was packed with an appreciative audience, which included some of the Lords Commissioners of the Admiralty, members of the Navy League, and many representatives of the Press … great applause greeted one particular film taken from the Warner lightship of yachts racing in rough weather. They came so close to the camera that, smothered in foam, they appeared to be sailing right out of the picture, and the effect on one member of the audience was so realistic that he was forced to leave suffering from acute sea-sickness!

As recreation moved onto the water in the late nineteenth century, yachting became an increasingly popular pursuit. At one level were small rowing boats and sailing gigs, at the other extreme were pioneering racing yachts and the luxury motor launches of the millionaire enthusiasts. The first Yacht Club in the world was founded in 1815 over rum and claret in the Thatched House Tavern in London by a group of gentlemen interested in sailing. They began meeting twice a year to share sea stories over dinner. Nelson's captain at Trafalgar, Thomas Hardy, headed a list of the naval members. In 1833 the sailor King, William IV, joined and renamed the club the Royal Yacht Squadron and before long they were organising contests at their annual regatta at Cowes in the Isle of Wight. The New York based schooner *America* won the 53-mile race around the island in 1851 and the America's Cup was born. Now contested at locations all over the globe, it continues to be the world's most prestigious yacht challenge.

The Yacht Racing Association was founded in 1876 and the first Round Britain race was held to celebrate Queen Victoria's Golden Jubilee in 1887. Venturesome sailors from the New York Yacht Club soon made daring midwinter crossings of the Atlantic, though

the first ocean race to be regularly held was the 300-mile Dover-Heligoland introduced by the German Kaiser in 1897 to celebrate Victoria's Diamond Jubilee. By the 1890s dry-plate technology had developed, with briefer exposure times and lighter equipment, allowing dedicated photographers to get close to their maritime subjects when they were at their most dramatic – moving quickly through the water with full sails set. 'Photographing fast steamers from a small boat, on the open sea, is a very difficult operation', one reviewer described, 'the perplexities of which can, to a great extent, be overcome by pluck and perseverance … the trick then is to aim at the ship and expose like lightning'.

On the waters of the West Atlantic, men like Nathaniel Stebbins, Henry Peabody and Willard Jackson of Boston or Charles Bolles, John Johnston and James Burton of New York, were all drawn by the artistic challenge, not to mention the 'spice and danger', of shooting from small boats as vast sailing yachts careered by. The marine environment was exceptionally hostile to these photographers. Sand, salt water and spray ruined unprotected equipment; light bouncing off the water would trick exposure meters; wind and boat movement would frequently blur the image. Waves and surf were so hazardous that they had to become expert boat handlers in their own right. In 1920, Morris Rosenfeld purchased his first chase boat, *Foto*, to keep up with the fastest yachts. His *Foto III*, designed by powerboat guru Frederick Lord, gave Rosenfeld the speed and maneuverability to anticipate photo opportunities and take his camera closer to the action as never before. Frank Beken, facing great yachts approaching at the speed of a train, used a rubber bulb gripped between his teeth to trigger his camera's shutter.

ABOVE: Pioneering marine photographer Frank Beken shooting from his motor-launch in the Solent, 1930.

LEFT: A selecton of photographs from the golden age of yachting. From top left to bottom right: The J-class racing yachts *Shamrock V* and *Astra*, by Frank Beken, 1931; Going aloft to furl the mainsail on square-rigger *Parma*, by Alan Villiers, 1933; *Mohawk* racing at the Royal Southampton Yacht Club Regatta, by Alfred John West, 1884; Emperor Wilhelm II's racing yacht *Meteor* runs aground in Osborne Bay in 1897 and is photographed by Frank Beken. The boat had touched down in a light wind and the crew are seen using their weight on the bowsprit to lift the keel out of the sand; Schooner *Migrant's* headsails, by Rosenfeld and Sons, 1934; *Sonya* leading the 15-metre class, by Frank Beken, 1911.

The swansong of the ocean-going sailing ship also coincided with the availability of portable, easy-to-use photographic equipment. Many seafarers, such as Captain Woodgate of the famous clipper *Cutty Sark*, took cameras with them, and some were able to capture spectacular images. Men such as Frank Hurley and Herbert Ponting on their voyages to Antarctica took marine photography to new levels of drama and expertise, revolutionising both the art and imagination of exploration. Yet, to my mind the finest to take his camera to sea was the Australian-born journalist Alan Villiers. He gained his first experience on a pioneering Antarctic whaling trip in 1923 and soon realised the visual potential of the majestic ships that carried grain from southern Australia to Europe via Cape Horn. In 1927, he joined the German windjammer *Herzogin Cecilie*, and described its thrilling race against the Swedish barque *Beatrice* in his first bestseller, *Falmouth for Orders*. In 1929, he signed on with the *Grace Harwar*, the last full-rigger in the Australian trade, and sailed for England again. Huge seas rose to greet her as she attempted to pass through Cook Strait:

When the wind returned it was from the east again, with fog, rain, and gale in succession. Oilskins were useless. There was no dry spot in the ship, nor a dry rag to wear. The forecastle was washed out time and time again. When the forecastle doors were shut, the air was stifling. When they were open, great seas swept joyously in. We kept them shut, preferring suffocation to exposure.

On both trips Villiers took a Kodak 120 camera with just two settings. Later, he was modest about his photographs: 'If there is any excellence in them, the credit is due to the foolproof qualities of the modern cheap camera, and not to the skill of the photographer'. Yet many of his images were superb, depicting the privations of the voyages, the motley bands of semi-outcast men who crewed the ships, and the terror and grandeur of storms in the Southern Ocean and Atlantic.

Versatile and resourceful, Villiers was also a superb writer and brought both knowledge and pleasure to millions who might never sail themselves but who shared his love for the sea. His photography was a form of poetry, a eulogy to the ocean. He inspired a generation of sailors and conservationists, long before green issues reached political debate – 'for was the wind not free?' In describing the Cape Horn ships as 'the most splendid blend of utility and sea strength and functional beauty ever achieved by European man', his romantic agenda

was clear. Like others before him, his marine photography had a purpose. By the 1920s, more and more vessels were incorporating modern refinements – steel masts and spars, enclosed wheelhouses and winches to work the sails – that enabled owners to cut manning levels to a minimum. He feared that the skills of seamanship were at an end. Villiers wanted to commemorate something almost elemental; 'the age-old encounter of man and the sea', a period of sea-faring that was, he felt, entering its twilight. The modern fleet had long since steamed past, racing on the ocean highway to all corners of the globe.

For a long time too the oceans would resist this change; remaining vast, powerful, out of reach, untameable. When Emily Dickinson wrote in 1873 that 'to multiply the harbours does not reduce the sea', she referred to the constancy of love, but taken literally her metaphor should in fact now alarm us. Though it would seem that man's activity on land and sea could have little effect on so large a world, we now know that the reverse is true. The balance of the oceans has been altered greatly by our actions, but the damage may not be irreparable. Returning the oceans to health this century may yet ensure our survival into the next.

When Captain James Cook landed on Hawaii in 1778 he was amazed by a strange sight at the beach. Men with 'oval pieces of plank' were riding waves that 'sent them in with a most astonishing velocity'. This was the first recorded account of surfing, long before photography, film, and now the Internet, would make mega-stars of the best surfers in the world. Cook's final Pacific voyage in *Resolution* also conducted some of the first examinations of marine life and deposits from the ocean floor, a process that is now possible remotely by submersible vehicles with findings beamed by satellite to shore-based command centres. Today, inventors are creating winged submarines with miniature cameras that stream live footage as they fly silently through the deep, exploring shipwrecks or following the great whales on their ocean migrations. In just 170 years of photographic innovation, from daguerreotype to digital, images have been created from the seashore to the surface of the moon and beyond, but most of our blue planet has never been glimpsed. Photography provides a snapshot of our relationship with the oceans. There is still much for us to see, and so much more to learn.

Cambridge, 2010

RIGHT: The *Lusitania* arriving in New York after her maiden voyage in 1907. She was the largest ocean liner in service at the time and would go on to make 202 Atlantic crossings on the Cunard Line's Liverpool-New York Route. She was torpedoed in 1915 by a German U-boat and she sank off the coast of Ireland with a loss of 1,198 lives, including almost a hundred children.

OCEAN PORTRAITS

The shouts of sailors double near the shores;
They stretch their canvas, and they ply their oars.

VIRGIL, *Aeneid,* **BOOK III**

Photography records the gamut of feelings
written on the human face, the beauty of the
earth and skies that man has inherited; and the
wealth and confusion that man has created. It is
a major force in explaining man to man.

EDWARD STEICHEN, 1955

I send thee a shell from the ocean beach;
But listen thou well, for my shell hath speech.
Hold to thine ear,
And plain thou'lt hear
Tales of ships...

CHARLES HENRY WEBB, *With a Nantucket Shell,* **1901**

GALLERY

OCEAN PORTRAITS

HUW LEWIS-JONES

This is a gallery of one hundred remarkable people; an album of lives shaped and inspired by the sea. It is neither complete nor definitive. Coming face to face with a selection of individuals in this way, we hope to celebrate the range of human activity above and below the waves and to reflect upon the future for our ocean world.

Though the history of humankind's relationship with the ocean can be read in many ways, photography provides us with a glimpse of more recent ambition and adventure. We have gathered together some of the finest images from the world's leading maritime collections, while creating striking new portraits of interesting and inspiring characters whose hopes and dreams are connected to the ocean.

We may meet battle-weary veterans or a storm-torn mariner, fresh from the fray. Or, perhaps, an ocean entrepreneur, enriched by trade from other lands. Cabin-boys, merchants, captains and stowaways – some eager to escape home, others happy to be safely returned. Eccentrics and visionaries, brave navigators and dedicated fisherfolk, deep-sea divers, film-makers, archaeologists, champion surfers, famous artists and authors, parents, daughters and sons; generations of souls, drawn to the sea.

We see men and women of many nations who have broadened the horizons of our understanding; scientists and educators, explorers and pioneers, all willing to try something extraordinary. Encounter inventors and innovators who have revolutionised the way we travel on, or even within, the ocean. Join a long-distance swimmer or an open-boat rower pushing themselves to the limits of what is thought possible, and beyond. We sit with famous skippers who race upon the wind, breaking records, pursuing fame, maybe doing it to disappear from the world or, simply, sailing for the challenge and the freedom it brings. Discover a lifeboatman willing to risk his life for another, with no mind for reward or renown. And, we listen to modern-day advocates for ocean conservation and hope that their message will be heard.

Cambridge, 2010

PREVIOUS PAGE: Ready for the next time the Achill Island lifeboat is called to sea, the crew's all-weather gear is neatly stowed in the boat house, 2008. Battling through the wild Atlantic storms that lash the west coast of Ireland, in just ten years of service here lifeboat crews have won eight awards for gallantry.

COWES, 1935

FRANK BEKEN 1880-1970

For a steady shot in rough seas, Frank William Beken held his large, mahogany box camera with both hands and used a small rubber ball clenched between his teeth to release the shutter. It was 'the size of a bread bin, and the weight of a typewriter' but it produced some of the finest marine photographs ever taken.

His father Alfred was a chemist who moved to the Isle of Wight in 1888, taking over a pharmacy business. When he wasn't helping in the shop, young Frank was out on the waters of the Solent, photographing magnificent yachts and ships of all kinds of sizes – from stately ocean liners and navy battleships to local pleasure craft. Frank developed his prints in his bedroom, and his window also provided the light source for his 'daylight powered enlarger', which enabled him to make saleable prints from his negatives. A new business was born. Due to Queen Victoria's residence nearby at Osborne, Cowes became the fashionable centre of the yachting community. Visiting royalty were a regular sight in the town and on one occasion, so family legend goes, five crowned heads of Europe visited the pharmacy at the same time. Among so many notable images, it is worth remembering that Frank took the last professional photograph of the immense RMS *Titanic*, as she sailed from Southampton on her maiden voyage in 1912. Recognizing him, Captain Edward Smith sounded the horn as he passed.

Frank's charismatic portrait was taken by his son Keith, who became a master marine photographer in his own right. 'Beken and Son' captured on glass plate and film some of the best-known yachts in the world, including King George's *Britannia*, Thomas Lipton's *Shamrock V*, and T.O.M. Sopwith's America's Cup legend *Endeavour*. On one occasion, Keith towed Prince Philip after his Dragon-class yacht *Coweslip* nearly sank. He later photographed all three of the Prince's yachts – *Coweslip, Bluebottle* and *Bloodhound* – during the 1950s and 60s, and was awarded a Royal Warrant. The Prince commented: 'I have an unjustified reputation for not liking photographers but the Beken camera is one I always welcome'. At the same time, Keith turned to colour, using his own home-made camera, and began to attend international regattas, particularly St Tropez in October, and in Antigua in the West Indies where the yachts used to do battle each spring. After Frank's death in 1970, Keith sold off the pharmacy part of the business and his son Kenneth joined the firm, which was renamed Beken of Cowes.

Keith Beken had an artist's eye, technical genius and a formidable memory. He could recognise yachts from miles away across the Solent by the length of their hull, the rig and the design of their sails and spinnakers. He continued to take pictures afloat into his eighty-sixth year, when he reluctantly decided to watch from the shore. He continued as an active part of the family business right up to his death, in 2007. He put his longevity down to 'drinking a pint of Guinness every day for sixty years and to breathing the salt of the sea all his life'.

PARIS, 2005
ELLEN MACARTHUR 1976-

Dame Ellen Patricia MacArthur is, perhaps, the most famous female sailor in the world. In 2005, just a few weeks before this portrait was taken, she had broken the record for the fastest solo circumnavigation of the globe, capturing the hearts and admiration of millions in the process. Though her time of 71 days, 14 hours, 18 minutes 33 seconds, was eventually bettered by the masterly French mariner Francis Joyon in 2008, MacArthur was among the first to congratulate him. 'It's just huge', she told the throng of reporters that morning in Brest, as Joyon was swallowed by the welcoming crowd: 'I really had to give everything I had to beat his 2004 record; today he betters mine by 14 days. Amazing seamanship, ideal weather and a faster boat are the key factors, but above all I cannot express how much respect I have for the man'.

Though she had been sailing since childhood, MacArthur first became more widely-known in 1997 after completing the Mini Transat, a solo trans-Atlantic race. She had fitted out her 21-foot yacht *Le Poisson* herself while living in a French boatyard. In 2000, she sailed the monohull *Kingfisher* from Plymouth to Newport, Rhode Island, in 14 days, 23 hours and 11 minutes, a female solo record that still stands. The following year she finished second in the Vendée Globe. But it was the stellar, record-breaking solo voyage on the trimaran *B&Q* in 2005 that secured her status as one of the greatest ocean racers. Among countless honours, she was awarded the *Legion d'honneur* and made ISAF World Sailor of the Year for her efforts. But in 2009, much to everyone's surprise, she announced her intention to retire from the sport to concentrate on environmental campaigning. Time will tell if she meets with the same success as an advocate for the ocean as she did racing on it, but it would be hard to find a more inspiring and committed individual than Ellen.

WASHINGTON, 1907
JOSHUA SLOCUM 1844-1909

Nova Scotia-born Joshua Slocum was one of the world's finest mariners. His grandfather was a lighthouse keeper, his father made leather boots for local fishermen, and as one of eleven children he found early life chaotic and restrictive. Yearning for adventure, he made several attempts to run away from home. At the age of fourteen he shipped as a cabin boy on a fishing schooner, but was soon returned to his parents when found out. Following the death of his mother, he left home for good and joined a merchant ship bound for Dublin. From Ireland he crossed to the busy port of Liverpool and found a berth on another merchant ship on its voyage to the trade in China. He twice rounded Cape Horn, and quickly rose through the ranks to become a Chief Mate on grain transport ships out of San Francisco.

In 1865 he became a US citizen. After some years fur trading in the Oregon, he returned to sea as a schooner pilot. His first blue-water command, in 1869, was the barque *Washington*, which he took across the Pacific. He continued as the master of at least eight other vessels, bringing precious cargoes back from the Spice Islands and Australia. He married in 1871, and over the next thirteen years his adventurous and understanding wife Virginia bore him seven children, all at sea or in foreign ports. Enduring shipwreck in Alaska, bouts of tropical disease and battles with pirates in the South Seas, the Slocum family travelled together across the oceans of the world, before moving to the east coast of America.

On the morning of 24 April 1895, Slocum weighed anchor in a fair wind, and sailed away from Boston in the little sloop *Spray*. 'A thrilling pulse beat high in me', he later wrote, 'my step was light on deck in the crisp air. I felt that there could be no turning back'. More than three years later, he returned to Rhode Island having circumnavigated the world, a distance of more than 46,000 miles. He tied the boat to the same cedar spike in the bank that had held her at her launch. 'I could bring her no nearer to home', he said. His classic book of this epic voyage, *Sailing Alone Around the World*, won him widespread fame. The celebrated author Arthur Ransome went so far as to declare, 'Boys who do not like this book ought to be drowned at once'.

This rare photograph is one of the last of Slocum. He sits on the cabin roof of *Spray*, moored in the Potomac River when visiting Washington in 1907. By 1909, Slocum's funds were running low; book revenues had slowed and he prepared to sell his farm on Martha's Vineyard, making plans for a new adventure to South America, exploring the Amazon and Orinoco rivers. 'I'm an old man, and I should like once more to feel a deck under my feet before it is too late', he said to a friend shortly before sailing south. In November, bound for the Cayman Islands, Slocum and *Spray* disappeared, never to be seen again.

SOUTH PACIFIC, 1978
BERNARD MOITESSIER 1925-1994

Master-mariner, environmental activist, author and sometime spiritual guru, Bernard Moitessier takes a sight at the mast of his beloved yacht *Joshua*. In 1968, the 'sea vagabond' as he was known, reluctantly set sail in the *Sunday Times* Golden Globe Race, in a bid to become the first to circumnavigate the earth alone and non-stop. It was not a happy beginning – he had been preparing to make the voyage before, by his own reckoning, the newspaper had jumped on the idea. He was outraged that his pure challenge between man and sea had been turned into a competition. 'Racing is an insult to the ocean!' he later declared.

Nonetheless, away he went and the world's press waited for news. He refused to have a radio onboard, instead using a catapult to shoot used film canisters containing scribbled messages to passing ships. Seven months into the race, and with a very good chance of winning, he continued on to Polynesia rather than making his way up the Atlantic. His decision to abandon the lead, sailing onward for three more months instead of returning to the media circus, made him a hero to many. After his 37,000-mile voyage, he wrote *The Long Way*, now regarded as the classic narrative of blue-water sailing. But his peace came not in the pages of a book, but out on the open ocean. 'My real log is written in the sea and sky; it can't be photographed and given to others'.

Though it's a title he would not have craved, Moitessier was surely one of the greatest sailors of all time. Of his refreshing, some may say eccentric, approach to life, he famously once said, 'you do not ask a tame seagull why it needs to disappear from time to time toward the open sea. It goes, that's all'.

ATLANTIC OCEAN, 1934
SIR THOMAS SOPWITH 1888-1989

Sir Thomas Octave Murdoch Sopwith, or 'T.O.M.' for short, was a pioneering aviator and celebrated yachtsman. His portrait was captured by Morris Rosenfeld, marine photographer extraordinaire. Sopwith, pipe in mouth, is at the helm of his magnificent J-class cutter *Endeavour*. It was 1934, the beginning of his first challenge of the America's Cup. In the second race Sopwith, the first British owner to skipper the boat himself, beat the course record. Later that year *Endeavour* was almost lost in a hurricane and with war looming she was put to bed in a mud berth.

Sopwith was born in 1888, the eighth child (hence the Octave) to parents of seven girls. Restless, energetic and with a penchant for dangerous antics, he gave his sisters merry hell. At fourteen he learnt to fly a balloon. He made his first flight, and first crash, in 1910. Undaunted, he taught himself on a British Avis monoplane and soon afterwards won a huge prize for a flight across the English Channel. In the next few years he made more than $28,000 by stunt-flying in America and returned home with his winnings to set up the Sopwith School of Flying at Brooklands. Soon afterward he began to manufacture aircraft. In 1912, he won the first aerial Derby and in 1913 a machine of his design, a tractor biplane, achieved the altitude record. His single-seat biplane fighter, the Sopwith Camel, proved a huge success on the Western Front in 1917, amid the desperation of that theatre of conflict. Bankrupt after the war, he rebuilt his business and continued to create some of the most exciting, and effective, aircraft the world has ever seen. The Hawker Hurricane and Supermarine Spitfire were instrumental in winning the Battle of Britain and securing peace for Europe.

Sopwith first challenged the America's Cup with his *Endeavour*. Designed by Charles Nicholson, with Sopwith's aeronautical engineer Frank Murdoch assisting with the rigging, she won the first two races impressively. In the third, which turned the Cup ultimately in America's favour, wily Sherman Hoyt mastered the light breeze and left *Endeavour* in his wake. Despite some controversy over the 1934 match, Sopwith returned in 1937 with *Endeavour II* but was soundly beaten by the superlative *Ranger*. Sopwith lived to see countless other America's Cup exchanges. Though he was beaten at sea, his aircraft ruled the skies. He died in Hampshire in 1989, aged 101, just months before his beloved *Endeavour*, rescued from obscurity, had been restored to the waves.

NEWPORT, 2010

ELIZABETH MEYER 1953-

Covered in wood shavings from a boat in the making, Elizabeth Ernst Meyer thinks her appearance 'totally ridiculous' but she is happy to humour us. We are down at the quayside in Newport, Rhode Island, at the International Yacht Restoration School, which she founded in 1993. Since then, the school has restored over 150 classic boats. Meyer is most well-known for rescuing the superlative *Shamrock V* and *Endeavour* J-class yachts from decay and returning them to their ocean-going glory.

In 1989, she was named *Yachting Magazine's* Sailor of the Year and was most recently awarded an Honorary Doctorate from Roger Williams University for her commitment to these beautiful craft. It is on the water, however, that Meyer is really able to appreciate her successes. While sailing *Endeavour* in San Diego harbour, she tells me, they overtook a 40-foot cruising boat called *Easy Rider*: 'It was all painted black, and even her crew were dressed in black tee shirts, scruffy jeans and cowboy boots. They didn't hear us coming and were shocked when we sprinted past them. Their helmsman almost fell overboard in surprise and yelled out, "YEEEEHA!" That's the ass-kickenest boat I ever seen! I knew immediately that we had done the right thing by bringing the beautiful *Endeavour* back to life'.

BOSTON, 1854
DONALD McKAY 1810-1880

Louis Daguerre's pioneering photographic process spread rapidly round the world after it was presented to the public in 1839. Exposed in a camera obscura and developed in mercury vapors, each highly-polished silvered copper plate was a unique image. This whole-plate daguerreotype of Donald McKay is one of the finest 'ocean' portraits, with extraordinary clarity for such an early work. The reason, no doubt, was down to the technical artistry of its makers, the celebrated Boston-based studio photographers Southworth and Hawes. McKay liked the portrait so much he had a copy hung in the captain's cabin of his new clipper ship.

McKay, a wealthy shipbuilder, native to Nova Scotia, joined the long line of America's elite who rushed for portraits in this fashionable studio. McKay's portrait is a statement of his rise in the world, of his strength and business success: energy that was turning the new nation into a mercantile superpower. 'Mr. McKay', one newspaper would report, 'delights in his noble profession, and considers labor or expense nothing, compared with success. It is his ambition to build the best, most beautiful, and swiftest clippers in the world'.

His first, *Stag Hound*, was launched in 1850. It was followed by many others including *Lightning*, the behemoth *Great Republic*, and the extreme clipper *Flying Cloud*, which sped across the oceans during the California Gold Rush. *Champion of the Seas* became the largest sailing vessel in the world when she was launched in 1854. She was also one of the fastest. In a period of 24 hours, in December 1854, she sailed some 465 nautical miles, a record which stood for over a century.

By 1860, the demand for huge clipper ships was declining and McKay was forced to suspend operations. In 1863, he re-equipped his yard to build iron ships for the US Navy, but it proved a costly and unrewarding exercise. He returned to sailing ships with the *Glory of the Seas*, which he funded himself and completed in 1869. It would be one of his most famous creations, but it was also his last for she bankrupted him. McKay was eventually overwhelmed by his creditors, to whom he owed close to $250,000 – an astronomical sum in 1870. Once one of the most celebrated naval architects the oceans had ever seen, he was left with only a few cents to his name.

SOUTH ATLANTIC, 2001
WILFRIED ERDMANN 1940-

The celebrated German yachtsman and author captures his self-portrait while in the South Atlantic during his non-stop voyage round the world. Sailing against the wind from Cuxhaven, he successfully returned to port after 343 days at sea. It was his third solo voyage – between 1966 and 1968, in the 25-foot *Kathena*, he became the first German to sail alone round the world, and in 1985 he became the first to sail non-stop around the world, from west to east, from Kiel to Kiel in just 271 days.

Born in Scharnikau, Erdmann went to school in East Germany before managing to escape to the West. In 1958 he embarked on his first solo adventure – on a bicycle – pedalling from Europe through northern Africa and the Middle East to Persia. He remembers being overwhelmed when he first caught sight of the sea on the Cote d'Azur. Later, meeting a sailor on the coast of Kerala in India, he knew that the ocean was calling him. One word, he recollects, inspires him more than any other and it's something he feels the sea provides: 'freedom'. After five years in the merchant navy, he decided to pursue his yachting dreams. In the decade following his brilliant first voyage, Erdmann also made two full circumnavigations joined by his wife Astrid and their young son Kym, and more journeys would follow. When asked, among a life so full of adventure and achievement, of the things for which he is most proud, his answer is quick: 'For forty years of sailing without needing rescue, or damaging the environment – and most important of all, for being at the right place at the right time in 1966, the wonderful year I found my wife in the port of Gibraltar!'

BOSTON, 1885
ROBERT FORBES 1804-1889

Captain Robert Bennet Forbes is pictured proudly in his studio at home, surrounded by the model ships he has made. A sedate retirement, perhaps, which belied a dramatic career as a master-mariner, entrepreneur, trader in fine art, diplomat and opium smuggler. Forbes began his colourful ocean life at the age of thirteen as ship's boy on a voyage to the East Indies. When his father's business failed young Forbes entered the employ of his uncles, James and Thomas Perkins, who were among the most successful New England merchants of the early nineteenth century. He became part of a network of prominent American families, whose energy overseas shaped the maritime history of this Golden era of sailing ships.

For more than twenty years, Forbes represented business interests in China, and his huge wealth grew as trade with the Far East flourished. He was a part owner of sixty-eight vessels, including the first paddle steamer on the Yangtze River. Forbes settled in Canton, exporting Chinese silks, earthenware and teas to America, and importing large quantities of silver, sandalwood, furs and other manufactured goods into the region, while also smuggling vast quantities of narcotics up river. When the First Opium War broke out in 1839, Forbes refused to leave his business interests: 'I had not come to China for health or pleasure, but that I should remain at my post as long as I could sell a yard of cloth or buy a pound of tea'. He did booming business until the British closed the harbour. As the markets in China became hostile and increasingly competitive, the Forbes family turned its attentions to the railroads and risked their fortune in backing Alexander Graham Bell's telephone company. The risk paid off.

With wealth amassed largely through the opium trade, in his leisured comfort Forbes was an inventor of life-saving equipment, a yachtsman, and a prolific writer of pamphlets on subjects ranging from ocean safety and historic ships, to the science of magnetism. Once a drug dealer, now re-invented humanitarian, he commandeered the USS *Jamestown* to send food to Irish famine sufferers in 1847 and became an ardent supporter of sailor's relief organisations. In gentle old age he took up watercolour painting and model shipbuilding.

QINGDAO, 2009
TORBEN GRAEL 1960-

Ericsson 4 skipper Torben Schmidt Grael arrives in Qingdao in freezing foggy conditions, during the latest Volvo Ocean Race. By June, having covered 42,500 miles across some of the toughest waters on the planet, Grael's team had secured overall victory. They had also smashed the monohull 24-hour distance record, sailing 596.6 nautical miles at an average of 24.85 knots. It had been an exhausting race for this most experienced of ocean skippers.

Born in São Paulo, Grael was first introduced to the sea by his grandfather, sailing on the 6-metre class *Aileen* on Guanabara Bay. Nicknamed 'Turbine' for his speed on the water, Grael would in time go on to win countless Continental and World Championships in the Snipe dinghy and Star keelboat classes. A five-time Olympic medallist and long regarded as one of the best all-round sailors of his generation, Grael was named ISAF World Sailor of the Year in 2009.

Despite these sailing accolades, he is most proud of the work he shared with his brother Lars, in setting up the Instituto Rumo Náutico, known in Brazil as 'The Grael Project'. Their dream was of a programme to give young people from low-income families the opportunity to learn how to sail while also gaining essential professional skills for later life. Supported by UNESCO, their visionary project continues to grow and has now directly helped over 10,000 children. 'The ocean means everything to us', Grael tells me. 'The wind has taken me to places I could never imagine. It has enabled me to follow my dreams, and it's a pleasure to have helped others on the way'.

NEWPORT, 1903
CHARLES BARR 1864-1911

A studio has been hastily erected in a Newport parlour to catch a photograph of one of the most respected skippers afloat. In this recently-discovered portrait, Captain Charlie Barr sits patiently in his uniform. He looks keen to be back out on the water. Barr was a modest fellow, rarely captured on camera, nor often at home in fact. The photographer James Burton was lucky to spend some time with a man who became one of the greatest sailors in the world.

Barr was born in Gourock, Scotland and in the early years supported his family by working as a grocer's boy and fisherman. He spent a hard winter on a flounder trawler out of the Clyde, and though the experience may have put others off the sea for life, Barr was in his element. In 1884, he took a job with his older brother John, delivering the yacht *Clara* to America where they raced her that summer. Their success was such that John was selected to skipper the America's Cup challenger *Thistle* for the Royal Clyde Yacht Club. Charlie served as a member of the crew and though their yacht was soundly beaten by *Volunteer*, his quiet modesty and huge ability drew him influential supporters. His international racing career had begun.

America attracted 'Wee Charlie', as he was affectionately known, and he soon became a citizen. Small he may have been, but there was nothing diminutive about his sailing prowess. No man would stand higher in the sport. He went on to command what seemed a continuous line of winning yachts, before his rise to fame brought him to the attention of the New York Yacht Club. When a champion skipper was wanted to command *Columbia*, against the first *Shamrock* challenge in 1899, Barr was the man. It was no real surprise the America's Cup stayed firmly in the host's trophy cabinet. He administered the same treatment to the second *Shamrock*, again in the *Columbia*, in 1901. In 1903, when this portrait was taken, he was the winning skipper with *Reliance*, perhaps the most famous, and formidable, of the Nathanael Herreshoff super-yachts. Barr finished off this incredible run of victories in setting the record for the fastest ocean crossing by a sailing yacht in the legendary Kaiser's Cup trans-Atlantic race in 1905. For that type of craft, his record of 12 days, 4 hours and 1 minute, stood for almost 100 years.

On the morning of 24 January 1911, while having breakfast with his family in Southampton, he 'suddenly placed a hand upon his heart and with a cry of pain fell forward into the arms of his wife'. He had suffered a massive, and fatal, heart attack. *The New York Times* broke the story the following day, and the yachting community on both sides of the Atlantic mourned his loss. Barr's life was cut off in his prime. The year before, in the schooner *Westward*, he had won a haul of trophies in competition with Kaiser Wilhelm and other German yachts at Keil, Cuxhaven and Cowes. He made eleven starts, and secured eleven victories. The crowds that cheered him on that summer expected nothing else.

WEYMOUTH, 2009

BEN AINSLIE 1977-

As a triple Olympic Gold Medalist and three-time ISAF World Sailor of the Year, it is fair to say that Charles Benedict Ainslie is one of the best in the business. It's a cold day in December and the first time he has returned to Finn sailing since his successes at the Beijing Olympics. The picture is a quick one as he's keen to get back to his training. He arrived at Weymouth from Malaysia, where his *Team Origin* had been competing in the Monsoon Cup, the final round of the 2009 World Match Racing Tour, via media calls at the Paris Boat Show. His dinghy was fully rigged and ready to go.

Ainslie will be lucky to grab a few weeks of relaxation, before more race-training in Spain and the Louis Vuitton Trophy Regattas in New Zealand. Then there's the planning for a future America's Cup campaign and his preparation for the next Olympics. Welcome to the busy life of one of the best sailors in the world. But, what of a perfect day's sailing? 'Well,' he laughs, 'that would be out on the water with a 40-foot cruising boat, a bunch of really good mates and a few bottles of beer!'

HONOLULU, 1937
DUKE KAHANAMOKU 1890-1968

Duke Kahanamoku poses for press photographers before plunging into the water at a Hawaiian swimming gala. It is 1937 and the veteran Olympic swimmer – renowned for his prowess in the water and for his grace and humility on land – was by this stage something of a national treasure. 'The Big Kahuna' is now widely regarded as the founding father of the modern sport of surfing, its first global ambassador. He was the embodiment of the aloha spirit; loving, compassionate, and respectful of others. In 1999, *Surfer Magazine* crowned him the 'Surfer of the Century'.

His father was named 'Duke' in honour of Prince Alfred, Duke of Edinburgh, who visited Hawaii in the year of his birth. The younger 'Duke', as first son, inherited the name when he was born in 1890. A strong boy, Duke Paoa Kahinu Mokoe Hulikohola Kahanamoku would surf on a 16-foot board made from the wood of the koa tree. At an amateur swim-meet in 1911, in the salt water of Honolulu harbour, he clocked 55.4 seconds over 100 metres, smashing the world record. Easily qualifying for the US swimming team, he went on to win a gold medal in the 100-metre freestyle at the Stockholm Olympics. In 1920, in Antwerp, he won gold medals both in the 100 meters and the relay. Four years later, he finished with a silver medal, being narrowly beaten by Johnny Weissmuller, later hero of the *Tarzan* films.

Handsome, fit and bronzed, Duke was also destined for the movies, appearing in such Hollywood potboilers as the 1925 silent film *Lord Jim* and the adventure *The Isle of Sunken Gold*. True screen stardom eluded him, but he didn't really want it anyhow. Kahanamoku travelled the globe giving swimming exhibitions and raising money for the Red Cross. His surfing exhibition at Sydney's Freshwater Beach, just before Christmas in 1914, is widely regarded as the most significant day in the development of surfing in Australia. He attracted a frenzy of reporting and it would not be long before thousands of admirers had taken up the sport. While living in California in 1925 he rescued eight men from a fishing vessel that capsized in heavy seas while attempting to enter the harbour at Newport Beach. Using his surfboard, he was able to dash through the waves and bring people back to the shore. His efforts were hailed as 'the most superhuman surfboard rescue act the world has ever seen'. Thus was born the tradition of lifeguards having rescue surfboards at the ready. Kahanamoku had emerged as the world's consummate waterman, 'its fastest swimmer and foremost surfer, the first truly famous beach boy'.

NORTH POLE, 2007
LEWIS GORDON PUGH 1969-

Lewis Gordon Pugh, 'the Human Polar Bear', emerges from the ocean at the North Pole. He has just swum a kilometre, spending almost eighteen heart-crushing minutes in the frigid waters. It was his most ambitious adventure yet – an act of 'inspiring madness', as one newspaper put it. He did it, he tells me, to draw attention to the melting of the Arctic sea ice. Stepping out from the comfort of a Russian nuclear-powered icebreaker, dressed only in his Speedos, cap and goggles, Pugh ventured where no man had wanted to swim before. 'You know its going to be cold', he confides, 'but what you don't realise until you get to the Pole is that the water is so dark, so deep. I felt like I was diving into a giant pot of black ink'.

A maritime lawyer turned environmental adventurer, Pugh has undertaken many expeditions to raise awareness about the effects of climate change, from the Norwegian fjords and the low-lying islands of the Maldives, to swims round the Cape of Good Hope and across Lake Malawi. In 2006, he swam down the River Thames, making a brief stop at Downing Street to petition the Prime Minister. He most recently announced at the Clinton Global Initiative that he will swim across a glacial lake in the Khumbu, the valley in the shadow of Mount Everest, to highlight the melting of glaciers in the Himalayas. The ungenerous may say 'what's the point?' – some even deny the reality of climate change altogether – but Pugh is rightly unrepentant. His determination is commendable. At least he is willing to do *something* on our planet's behalf. 'I'm neither an adventurer, nor a tree hugger. I'm a new breed of hands-on, act-now activist. In the end, the most important thing is to follow your own dreams, because if you don't, you will end up following someone else's. Imagine getting to the end of your life and that were the case – nothing could be sadder.'

LONDON, 1845
HENRY LE VESCONTE 1813-1848

In 1845, Captain Sir John Franklin and his crews bade their farewells as their exploration ships *Erebus* and *Terror* slipped down the Thames, heading out on their scientific voyage into the Arctic and the unknown. They were last glimpsed later that summer, moored to an iceberg high in Lancaster Bay. They were never seen again. Over the coming decade, some thirty expeditions were sent out in search of the party. In 1859, the Irish explorer Leopold McClintock returned to London bearing terrible news. Along with recovered artefacts, he finally confirmed that Franklin and all his men had perished. The nation mourned their loss – it was one of the greatest tragedies in the history of exploration.

In the Old Royal Naval College, Greenwich, there is a monument to Sir John Franklin and those brave men who died alongside him. Designed by Royal Academician Richard Westmacott, it was erected by Order of Parliament in the Painted Hall in 1858. Following building work, it was moved to the Chapel in 1938, where it has recently been conserved for public display. A skeleton recovered from the Arctic wastes by American explorer Charles Francis Hall was identified by family members as Lieutenant Henry Le Vesconte of HMS *Erebus*. His bones were returned for entombment in the Monument in 1873, the only remains that ever made it home to England.

Henry Thomas Dundas Le Vesconte was born in Netherton, Devon, first son of a naval commander. He entered the Navy as a first-class volunteer on *Herald* in 1829 and won his lieutenancy by 'repeated acts of conspicuous gallantry' as Mate on the sixth-rate *Calliope* during the Opium War. He later served on the sloop *Hyacinth* in the East Indies and on *Clio* off the coast of Africa in cruises to suppress the slave trade. On 4 March 1845 he was made Second Lieutenant to the *Erebus* as she was fitting out for the polar expedition at Woolwich Dockyard.

Little is known of Le Vesconte's activity on this voyage. We know he sat for his portrait with the innovative photographer Richard Beard, as did other officers before they left London. This was the first, and the last, photograph to be taken of him. He sent a number of letters and sketches home, as *Erebus* headed north into Baffin Bay late in 1845. But after that, as with the expedition as a whole, few exact details survive. It is possible he endured the third winter and was alive into 1848 though the circumstances of his death are not known. A special memorial service, held in London in 2009, celebrated his life and the legacies of maritime exploration and discovery in the Canadian north.

LONDON, 2009
ROBERT GRENIER 1937-

Dr Robert Grenier speeds down-river on a Thames clipper catamaran. Grenier is Chief Marine Archaeologist for Parks Canada and the man that all polar history buffs are keen to meet. We are on our way to a special service at the Old Royal Naval College in Greenwich, a gala celebration of Arctic endeavour, and Grenier is due to speak. For now, we are pleased to be away from the crowds.

Grenier has devoted much of his eminent career surveying shipwrecks in the remote waters of our planet, but it is his recent search for the missing ships of Sir John Franklin's fateful expedition that has made him the focus of international attention. 'I would rather get on with the job in hand, you know', he confides, 'everyone seems to have an opinion about where they might be. For our own part, we are employing the old and the new – sensitively listening to Inuit testimony while also using icebreakers and sophisticated underwater survey techniques, so who knows what may be possible'. Some think the whole thing is a 'waste of money', particularly in this financial climate, while others suggest it is much more about Canada's sovereignty claims in the High Arctic than the desire for archaeological excellence. Whatever the critics may say, Grenier is rightly unapologetic. 'Yes, this may be the Holy Grail of shipwrecks if we find it, but equally there is something appealing in its mystery. It may be a gift, or a curse. We shall see'.

PORTSMOUTH, 1872
SIR GEORGE NARES 1831-1915

Vice Admiral Sir George Strong Nares, polar explorer and man of science, was the commander of the *Challenger* expedition from 1872 to 1874. It was a voyage of exploration and survey that, it has been said, 'laid the foundations of almost every branch of oceanography as we know it today'. Nares also found some literary fame as author of *Seamanship*, a guide to life afloat, which went through at least eight editions. His name was given to two capes in the Canadian Arctic, Mount Nares in Antarctica, and the Nares Deep in the north Atlantic. Though not well known today, his rich legacy is found written on charts the world over.

Born in Monmouthshire, Nares entered the Navy in 1845 as a prize cadet. He served on the Australian station as midshipman and mate, visiting for the first time a number of islands in the South Pacific and distinguishing himself in rescuing a man swept overboard. In 1852 he was appointed mate on HMS *Resolute*, as part of a squadron heading to the Arctic to search for Sir John Franklin. He took part in a number of sledge journeys until his ship was also abandoned in the ice. From 1865 he was in Australian waters, surveying in the paddle-steamer *Salamander*. He returned to the Mediterranean to survey the Gulf of Suez, shortly before the celebrated Canal opened, revolutionising ocean transport. He conducted more survey work in the Strait of Gibraltar, including new oceanographic research into currents; work that led to his appointment as captain of HMS *Challenger* for its pioneering oceanographic circumnavigation. This portrait was taken shortly before he took to the sea.

With the ongoing success of this voyage, he was recalled to take command of an ambitious expedition toward the North Pole in 1875. Though a new 'Farthest North' was reached, toiling by sledge across the frozen Arctic sea ice, his crews suffered scurvy and the expedition returned home early the following year. Despite failure, the British public embraced them as heroes. 'Overworked, overtired, borne down by the weight of a dreadful and depressing malady, cold, hungry, they struggled on', narrated one journal, 'and individual heroism stepped in to save the honour of the day!' Others were less enthused by the obvious failures of the voyage: 'Verily the expedition of 1875-76 has but little of which to boast. It went out like a rocket, and has come back like the stick'.

Nonetheless, in 1878 Nares was again in command of *Alert* during its survey of the Strait of Magellan, before moving to a post in the Harbour Department at the Board of Trade. He retired in 1886 but continued to take an active interest in exploration, helping plan several expeditions to the Southern Ocean and Antarctica. He was a 'most amiable, kind-hearted man, beloved by his men', modest in public, conscientious at work, and meticulous in his planning of exacting ocean surveys. He regarded his biggest success, however, his family of four sons and five daughters. His youngest son, John, later became Director of the International Hydrographic Bureau at Monaco – a fitting testament to his father's inspiring oceanographic work.

SAINT-MALO, 1986
FLORENCE ARTHAUD 1957-

French skipper Florence Arthaud relaxes in Saint-Malo just days before she departed in the 1986 Route du Rhum. Now famous, this trans-Atlantic single-handed yacht race takes place every four years from Brittany to Pointe-à-Pitre on the island of Guadeloupe. That year the race was eventually won by French master mariner Philippe Poupon. Arthaud returned for its next running in 1990 and stunned a field of thirty of the world's leading ocean racers to finish in first place, well clear of Poupon and the Swiss skipper Laurent Bourgnon. She was the first woman to win and, in a time of just 9 days, 22 hours and 5 minutes, it was also the fastest solo crossing yet made.

A version of this elegant portrait would soon make the front cover of *Paris Match* magazine. Nicknamed the 'sweetheart of the Atlantic' by an overjoyed French press, Arthaud's beauty belied her gritty toughness at sea. A few years later, as the favourite to win the solo Europe 1 Star trans-Atlantic race, she was knocked unconscious as her 60-foot trimaran *Premier 1er* capsized almost 400 miles from the finish line. It flipped over as she was sailing in heavy seas at 29 knots, a top speed then for multihulls. Dramatically rescued by a passing cargo ship, she was lucky to be alive.

The first woman to cross an ocean single-handed was Ann Davison, who set off from Plymouth in May 1952 in the 23-foot wooden sloop *Felicity Ann*. By way of Brittany, Portugal and the Canary Islands, she eventually touched land in Dominica the following year. In 1965, Sharon Sites Adams made history as the first woman to sail solo from mainland America to Hawaii and in 1969 she dared the crossing of the Pacific again, from Yokahama to San Diego. Champion French sailor Marie-Claude Faroux competed in the single-handed trans-Atlantic race in 1972, taking 33 days to make the crossing. In 1988, after 189 days at sea, Australian Kay Cottee cruised into Sydney becoming the first female sailor to complete a single-handed, non-stop circumnavigation of the world. All of these inspirational sailors deserve a place in this book, but it is Arthaud we have chosen to feature here. Her record-breaking ocean crossing in 1990 amazed many in the sport, though for those who knew her skill and courage it was no surprise. For a time her victory made her one of the most famous figures in France but the legacy of her achievement would be longer lasting: she had shown everyone, if any more proof were necessary, that the oceans were not just a man's world.

WHITBY, 1880
HENRY FREEMAN 1835-1904

On 9 February 1861, when Whitby's lifeboat capsized on duty, just one crewmember survived. Henry Freeman was the only man wearing the new cork lifejacket. This stunning portrait is by celebrated photographic artist Frank Meadow Sutcliffe. Freeman was a brick-maker who had turned to the sea and fishing after the decline of the trade. It was his first day volunteering in the lifeboat.

A storm had been building and when dawn broke the lifeboat was launched. By early afternoon, five crews had been saved from fishing boats caught in the gale and the lifeboatmen were exhausted by their battle with the raging seas. Two schooners were then seen being driven onto the shore, north of the piers. One of them succeeded in crossing the harbour bar to safety, but the other, the *Merchant*, began to drift toward the beach. The lifeboat crew put to sea again, pulling hard on their oars through the breakers but they capsized just fifty yards from shore. Twelve lifeboatmen drowned within sight of their distraught relatives, who were among the hundreds who watched helplessly from the beach. The greatest tragedy of all was that the men had lowered their lifebelts, because they had rowed so much that day their arms were ripped raw with chaffing.

Though devastated by the disaster, Freeman went on to honour his lost friends by spending more than forty years in the service. As coxswain for twenty-two years he saved countless lives. He became a respected ambassador for the lifeboat cause and a leading spokesman for his fellow fishermen. However, from his death in 1904 until 1986, when schoolboys raised the money for a tombstone, Freeman's grave in the Whitby cemetery remained unmarked and it is only recently that his ocean achievements have been acknowledged. A bronze sculpture of Freeman is now proudly displayed on the wall of Whitby's new lifeboat station, which opened in 2007. He wears his trusty cork lifejacket, together with a Staithes pattern fisherman's jumper and the silver medal for gallantry he was awarded after the tragedy. Overlooking the harbour, his weather-beaten face stares out past the piers, to the North Sea, the cause of so much heartbreak and heroism over the centuries.

RIO DE JANEIRO, 2009
MAGNUS OLSSON 1949-

Arriving in Brazil, veteran Nordic mariner Magnus Olsson celebrates winning Leg 5 of the Volvo Ocean Race. With his crew of *Ericsson 3*, they had just sailed over 12,300 miles from China. Sixty years old, he had defied the doubters to put in a stunning performance across the Pacific. For a long-time the 'unsung hero' of ocean racing, he was competing in his sixth circumnavigation as a crewmember before an injury to his skipper Anders Lewander meant he had to step up to the helm. Olsson had well deserved his time in the spotlight. 'I've come face-to-face with so many legendary sailors over the years', Rick Tomlinson tells me, 'but the best of the lot is certainly Magnus. It would be hard to meet a more honest, positive and inspiring bloke, he's really brilliant'. Everyone I have spoken to says much the same – he's a true ocean hero. Another friend agrees: 'Behind every great man there is a great woman, and behind every great skipper... Magnus!'

The Volvo Ocean Race in 2008-09 was the tenth running of this ocean marathon. Starting from Alicante in Spain, on 4 October 2008, for the first time, it took in Kochi, India, Singapore and Qingdao before culminating in St Petersburg. Spanning some 37,000 nautical miles, visiting eleven ports over nine months, it remains the world's premier ocean yacht race for professional crews. And Olsson, well, he's surely its most cheerful ambassador. The day this photograph was taken, he tells me, was the happiest of his life.

LIVERPOOL, 1914
WILLIAM TURNER 1856-1933

Captain William Thomas Turner was master of the great luxury ocean liner *Aquitania* and a distinguished Commodore of the Cunard Line fleet. Standing by the compass platform on the flying bridge, Turner is wearing the full dress uniform of a Commander in the Royal Naval Reserve and medals for courageous service. It is 1914 and *Aquitania* is about to leave Liverpool on her maiden voyage to New York. This photograph captures a fleeting moment of pride and happiness for the notoriously shy, veteran skipper. Little could he know the tragedy that would later consume him.

Born in Liverpool, the son of a sea captain, his parents actually wanted him to become a minister and have a 'respectable life'. Instead, he escaped to sea as a cabin boy, at just eight years old aboard the bark *Grasmere*. When she was later wrecked in a gale off Ireland, Turner refused the offer of help and swam ashore himself. Undeterred, he returned to the life at sea, taking passage in a clipper bound for the Guanape Islands off Peru. As second mate on the *Thunderbolt*, he was swept overboard on the way to Calcutta while fishing for dolphins. Turner was in the shark-infested water for two hours, but was eventually hauled to safety.

After such narrow escapes, its no surprise that Turner was a superstitious man – he bought a new hat before each voyage, and with it wore the nickname 'Bowler Bill'. He was quiet, somewhat surly in company, lacking the usual polish of the Cunard Captains. He found the First Class passengers a particularly tiresome lot: 'a load of bloody monkeys who are constantly chattering', he once said. He avoided dinner at the Captain's table preferring instead to take a plate of meat up on the bridge. Passengers began to find his rough character appealing and in no time people were signing up for cruises just to meet him. Baffled by this popularity, Cunard gave him command of *Carpathia* for the whole of 1904 and passenger revenues doubled. Irascible he may have been, but at sea he was a master. He was appointed to *Mauretania* for her maiden voyage, and went on to smash the trans-Atlantic speed records, while also rescuing the crew of a burning Liverpool steamer en route. Turner became the hero of the fleet, beloved by crew and passengers alike.

In December 1910, Cunard announced a Christmas special – a voyage from Liverpool to New York and back in just twelve days. Turner accomplished the record sailing despite being told it was impossible and he found himself the darling of the press. However, Turner is mostly remembered now for being in command of the liner *Lusitania*, the world's largest ship at the time, when she was torpedoed by a German submarine off the south coast of Ireland in 1915. Turner remained at his post throughout the ensuing chaos, giving instructions as best he could, as waves overtook the ship and her boilers exploded. Turner stayed on the bridge as she sank from under him. The crew of the steamer *Bluebell* later pulled him unconscious from the ocean. Miraculously, he was spotted floating in the water, despite thick fog, by the gold braid of his officer's uniform. Others, however, were not so lucky. Over a thousand passengers lost their lives that afternoon.

Though Turner was lucky to be alive, his career never recovered and he slipped into deep depression. For many years he lived as a recluse, unable to come to terms with the disaster. On the King's birthday and St. George's Day he would emerge at his home, flying the Union Jack from the flagpole in the garden and entertaining local children with sea-shanties and an old violin. Stricken with intestinal cancer, he quipped 'I'm all right fore and aft, but my longitudinal bulkhead's given way!' Though he had recovered something of his notorious sense of humour, the tragedy haunted him for the rest of his life.

MONTEREY, 1998
PHIL NUYTTEN 1941-

An internationally recognised pioneer in the diving industry, Dr René Theophile Nuytten has spent over forty years creating deepwater products that have revolutionised man's relationship with the sea. This undersea portrait shows Nuytten testing one of his micro-subs in the waters off California. A peerless inventor, he is also an author and an artist. *Saturday Night* magazine put it this way: 'Phil designs it, Phil builds it, Phil tests it, Phil gets to have all the fun. He says he's never really thought of himself as a kid, but he's never been anything else. There must have been some negligent – or indulgent – adult years ago, someone who didn't call him in when it was time to grow up'. Nuytten laughs at this and smiles, 'couldn't have said it better myself!'

Through his companies, Nuytco and Can-Dive, he has developed the technology to allow longer-length diving expeditions with increased safety. His one-atmosphere systems – the hard-suits *Newtsuit* and *Exosuit*, and his deep-diving *DeepWorker* submersibles – are renowned internationally and are standard in nearly a dozen navies. Contract work has taken him to oilfields, submarine construction sites and sunken wrecks around the world, including the *Breadalbane* where his record dives through icy Arctic waters earned him a place on the cover of *National Geographic*. Nuytten was one of the forces behind the 'Sustainable Seas Expeditions' in the 1990s, a five-year initiative to study deep ocean environmental impacts on marine sanctuaries. Their findings contributed significantly to our understanding of underwater biodiversity.

Nuytten and his team are currently training astronauts from NASA to pilot the *DeepWorker* submersibles. The Pavilion Lake Research Project will advance the long-term objective of planetary exploration by combining research on life in extreme environments with high fidelity training in an underwater, remote setting. The information gained will help to improve the tools and techniques of future human missions to the Moon, Mars and beyond. Much of the ocean too, remains undiscovered and men like Nuytten are explorers in every sense of the word. Or, as he modestly tells me, 'I just like to mess around with stuff I enjoy. The ocean is my muse, that's the serious comment, but it's really just a whole lot of fun'.

NEW JERSEY, 1899
JOHN HOLLAND 1840-1914

The Irish-American inventor John Philip Holland emerges from the miniature conning tower of his submarine *Holland VI*, alongside in the dock at Perth Amboy, New Jersey. After finally passing her sea trials, she would be commissioned as the USS *Holland*, at the dawn of a new century. Man of the church, turned patriot and entrepreneur, this pioneering marine engineer would change the face of ocean warfare forever.

The son of a coastguard, Holland was born in County Clare. Educated first at Limerick, he was prevented from going to sea by poor eyesight and looked destined for a life as a religious teacher. But in 1872 his family emigrated to America and he quit his job to join them. From an early age he was interested in inventions and soon hit upon the idea of a submersible boat. As an Irish patriot, he saw how they might be used against the ships of the Royal Navy in the fight for Irish independence. There had been numerous proposals for underwater craft throughout the century, but the technical problems were, at that time, insurmountable. By 1870, he had drawn up his first detailed plans to the stage where he felt confident in offering them to the US Navy, but his torpedo boat was rejected as the fanciful scheme of a lunatic landsman.

Supported by wealthy Irish republicans, Holland tested his first craft underwater in 1878. They gave him more money to build a full-size submarine, which they hoped could cross the Atlantic and single-handedly destroy the British fleet. The *Fenian Ram*, completed in 1881, dived to a depth of sixty feet but was later abandoned. In 1895, after many uncertain years, Holland was awarded a contract to build a sub for the US Navy. His first, the steam-powered *Plunger*, was not a success and with only $5,000 of his own capital left, he began to build the *Holland* to his own design, fifty-four feet in length and ten feet in diameter. It was fitted with a petrol engine to zip along at the surface and revolutionary electric storage batteries for running submerged. Armed with a reloadable torpedo tube and a pneumatic dynamite gun, the energetic, optimistic craft was launched in 1897 and after further tests was purchased by the US government. A few months later, six more were ordered, and within a short time Russia, Japan, and Britain wanted submarines of their own. His inventions precipitated an arms race between the industrialised nations. With the threat of war looming, his 'Electric Boat Company' was finally in business.

ALAMEDA, 2010
SYLVIA EARLE 1935-

Sylvia Earle welcomes us on the roof terrace at DOER Marine, amongst the wharves of Alameda, San Francisco. Inside the workshop of her company headquarters below us, undersea vehicles in various states of repair jostle for attention. A micro-submarine is parked in the foyer, idle and out of its element, as if somehow washed ashore. Like Sylvia herself, it seems keen to get back to the water. The sun is rising. There is work to be done, but adventure beckons.

Dr Sylvia Alice Earle was named *Time* magazine's first 'Hero for the Planet' in 1998, and was soon afterward inducted into the American Women's Hall of Fame. Affectionately crowned 'Her Deepness' by *The New Yorker*, Earle's work has been at the frontier of deep ocean exploration for four decades. She has led some seventy expeditions, logging more than 6,500 hours underwater. 'I've always wanted to get out in the sea', she tells me, smiling. 'We all want to see fish, real fish, not fish in a laboratory. I can still feel that leap of enthusiasm, and real joy, at the prospect of finally getting out on the ocean'.

The winner of numerous lifetime awards across the world – almost a hundred in all – Earle's most recent honour was in winning the TED Prize in 2009, as a visionary oceanographer and one of the environment's most prominent ambassadors. Receiving a million dollar grant, she plans to engage a worldwide audience to support marine protected areas. She calls these sanctuaries 'hope spots', places to save and restore the blue heart of the planet. 'If the sea is sick, we'll feel it. If it dies, we die. Our future and the state of the oceans are one'.

PARIS, 1970
JACQUES-YVES COUSTEAU 1910-1997

This French oceanographer, naval officer, environmental advocate and adventure broadcaster, opened up more of the Earth's surface to human endeavour than any other explorer. His superlative life defies easy categorization, but it was perhaps his energy, his insatiable curiosity and the ability to share his sense of wonder with those around him, that ensures him almost universal recognition. His passion for the oceans continues today through his family and the millions of people inspired by his work.

Jacques-Yves Cousteau was born in Saint-André-de-Cubzac, a small town near Bordeaux. He spent much of his childhood at the beach and, carefree and rebellious, he was expelled from school for breaking its windows. In 1930 he entered the École Navale and graduated as a gunnery officer. He had dreamed of a career as a French navy aviator until a near fatal automobile crash dashed those hopes, but serendipitously led him to his true vocation. Taking up swimming to strengthen his broken arms, Cousteau fell in love with the sea.

Before Cousteau, undersea exploration was limited by the length of a human breath or the tether on a diving helmet. With the engineer Émile Gagnan he perfected the Aqua-Lung, the revolutionary self-contained underwater breathing apparatus – better known by the acronym 'scuba' – that enabled him, in his own words, to fly through the sea like a 'manfish'. In 1950, he bought the former minesweeper *Calypso*, which he converted into a floating laboratory, outfitted with the latest undersea exploration and television gear. He took the ship to the Red Sea, where he shot the first colour footage ever taken at a depth of 150 feet, and embarked on an odyssey across the oceans of the world for more than four decades. The motto of his ship in its glory days became his lifelong credo: *Il faut aller voir*, 'we must go and see for ourselves'.

The first of his many books, *The Silent World*, detailed the development and promise of scuba diving. Published in 1953, it was an instant bestseller and made him an international celebrity. Cousteau went on to share his undersea adventures with millions of television viewers. Loyal audiences of his documentary series *The Undersea World of Jacques Cousteau*, came face to face for the first time with sharks, whales, dolphins, sea turtles, walruses, penguins and giant octopuses. They grew 'accustomed to the highly personal, Gallic-flavored English of the ubiquitous captain', whose 'deeply lined face, dazzling smile and red woolen watch cap' made him one of the most recognizable figures on television.

'When you dive', he once said, 'you begin to feel that you're an angel. Man has only to sink beneath the surface and he is free. Buoyed by water, he can fly in any direction – up, down, sideways – by merely flipping his hand. It's a liberation'. Cousteau would become the eloquent champion of the oceans. 'The future of civilization depends on water', he said shortly before he passed away, 'I beg you all to understand this'. This was the constant appeal he voiced throughout a career of campaigning on the planet's behalf. A life so full of achievement, with accolades and honours too many to mention, Cousteau has left a legacy to the oceans like no other. One only hopes that his message continues to be heard.

SANTA BARBARA, 2010
JEAN-MICHEL COUSTEAU 1938-

I talk with the prolific film-producer Jean-Michel Cousteau on the beach in California. Evening is fast approaching and Cousteau is about to fly to Europe. We are lucky to spend a few hours with this charismatic ocean advocate, for he is a busy man and there is much to do. 'There really must be a sense of urgency for the planet now, you know', he tells me. 'It's sad. It's no longer enough for us all to say we love the ocean – we need to act and to do something decisive. If we don't, it is *us*, not just the polar bears or the beautiful whales, that are in trouble. We are an endangered species. We've trashed the oceans, and in some ways we deserve what's coming. It's our turn next'.

Jean-Michel is the first son of ocean explorer Jacques-Yves Cousteau. Since being 'thrown overboard' by his dad at the age of seven with a newly-invented scuba on his back, Jean-Michael was destined for an ocean life. Despite the opportunities and the pressures of so famous a name, Jean-Michel has forged his own career to become a leading ambassador for the environment. In 1999 he founded the Ocean Futures Society, a non-profit conservation and education organization to champion the needs of the sea. His children Fabien and Celine often join him on his adventures, from the Amazon River to the waters of the Arctic, communicating to new generations their love and concern for our water planet.

In 2006, his documentary *Voyage to Kure* inspired the US government to protect over 140,000 square miles of ocean waters and atolls to the northwest of Hawaii, now called the Papahānaumokuākea Marine National Monument and one of the largest marine protected areas in the world. It's a huge achievement and one that his father would have admired. 'But it must only be the beginning of something far more ambitious', he says. 'Until we have seriously begun to protect huge areas of our oceans, then gestures like these will remain just gestures. Hope and action, that's what all of us need, now more than ever'.

MONHEGAN ISLAND, 1886
MILTON BURNS 1853-1933

The eccentric Milton James Burns was one of America's most acclaimed marine painters, and one of the few to have experienced being a sailor himself. One critic noted that he looked 'as much a mariner as he does an artist'. He served on fishing vessels all along the East Coast. His kept his whiskers long, told tall stories, sung shanties, swam naked, drank heartily, and was always out with his sketchbook before dawn.

During his most prolific period, from 1875 to 1899, he worked both as a painter and illustrator. In 1886, Burns made a voyage throughout the Caribbean with the author William Agnew Paton, and this recently-discovered photograph shows the artist posing for one of his future illustrations, at his summer studio on Monhegan Island. Burns recreates for the camera his mastery of a stubborn creole pony, gamely driven into the crater of St Lucia's Soufriere volcano, umbrella in one hand, his sketchbook in the other. The resulting book, *Down the Islands*, appeared in New York in 1887. Burns continued to travel widely, hoping to set up his own studio in Europe. While in France, in 1932, he became ill and died the following year in New York.

Burns was introduced to marine painting when he joined William Bradford's cruise to the Arctic in 1869. He returned to study at the National Academy of Design in New York and was a founding member of the adventurous Salmagundi Sketch Club. In the early 1870s young Burns also became friends with Winslow Homer and went with him on several sketching trips. They spent much of their time on sailboats, along the Maine coast and the Grand Banks. Burns and Homer shared the belief that the artist should go directly to nature for inspiration. One reviewer described his works: 'He painted them vividly and strongly, for he shared the perils of the life and mixed his oils with more than a dash of sea salt'. Burn's magazine commissions took him all over the world, living among the fisherfolk of France, Norway, the Pacific Northwest and the West Indies. 'Burns is much more than a painter or illustrator of fishing life', one admirer commented, 'he is the fisherman's friend, a devoted, understanding friend, his interpreter to the world'.

CONNEMARA, 2009
DOROTHY CROSS 1956-

Dorothy Cross sits in her studio on the west coast of Ireland, on a plot of land at the edge of the sea. Born in Cork, she studied in England and at the San Francisco Art Institute in the early 1980s. Her work moves from sculpture to film and photography. She is best known for representing Ireland at the Venice Biennale in 1992 and for her charismatic installation *Ghostship*, a phosphorescent disused lightship that was moored in Dublin Bay in 1999. She smiles, when recalling her first photograph of the ocean: 'Well, it was more my father's than mine. We went out to see the ocean liners that anchored off Cork harbour and did handstands on the deck for the American tourists. They threw Pall-Mall cigarettes and bananas at us'.

In 2002, Cross worked with her brother Tom, a Professor of Zoology and former national swimming coach, on *Medusae*, a film series about jellyfish. In the summer of 2005, the Irish Museum of Modern Art held a major retrospective of her remarkable career. From scuba-diving under icebergs in Antarctica, to learning from the shark-callers of Papua New Guinea, the ocean has provided Cross with a rich source of inspiration. Now creating sculptures from dead sharks and whalebone, she is also dreaming up a vast new installation, a six-metre submarine, gilded with pure gold-leaf and containing a human heart – a reliquary, perhaps, for our troubled relationship with the sea.

BALLYCOTTON, 1937
PATRICK SLINEY 1885-1972

Irishman Patrick 'Patsy' Sliney is chief among the very many courageous lifeboatmen that have come from that country. He finally retired in 1950, after forty years service to the lifeboat and saving 114 lives. He is famous for being the long-serving coxswain of Ballycotton's *Mary Stanford*, whose entire crew and the boat herself were awarded medals for gallantry at sea. Ballycotton is a small fishing village on Ireland's wind-swept Atlantic coast, set on a rocky ledge overlooking the sea.

In 1936, during the worst hurricane in living memory, the Daunt Rock lightship broke away from her moorings in the western approaches to Cork harbour. The seas were so large, that spray was seen flying over the lantern of the lighthouse, some two hundred feet in the air. The lifeboat was at sea for almost fifty hours and her crew had no food and just three hours sleep. She returned to the plunging vessel more than a dozen times with mountainous seas sweeping over her. It was one of the most perilous rescues in the history of the service, but not a single life was lost. When Sliney's crew returned home they were so tired they had to be lifted from their boat.

Sliney was awarded another medal in 1941 for rescuing sailors of the sinking ship *Primrose*, in thick fog through a heavy sea choked with mines. He was honoured again for going to the rescue of the steamship *Irish Ash*, braving vertiginous seas on Christmas Eve, 1942. Sliney came ashore covered in salt water burns, his hands bloodied and bruised, his wrists inflamed to twice their normal size and his voice completely gone. All thirty-five crew had been saved.

After witnessing the destruction of dozens of ships in these brutal Atlantic storms, and joining in rescues himself, Sir William Hillary appealed to the Navy and the government for better support for seafarers. The 'National Institution for the Preservation of Life from Shipwreck' was founded as a charity in 1824. Renamed the Royal National Lifeboat Institution in 1854, their crews and lifeguards have now saved more than 137,000 lives. The RNLI established a station at Ballycotton in 1858. The first lifeboat had eight crew and six oars, and was launched down the side of a steep cliff. The Daunt Rock has always been a hazard to shipping. The first lightship was stationed there in 1864, following the wreck of the *City of New York*. During a severe gale in October 1896 the lightship *Puffin* vanished. The wreck was discovered a month later, but the bodies of its crew were never recovered. It was in such treacherous conditions that generations of lifeboat men like Sliney ventured out to help those in peril on the seas.

KE IKI BEACH, 2009
CLARK LITTLE 1968-

Some ocean artists sketch on the beach, others visit for just a moment then spend their careers in a studio far from the sea. An adventurous few, like Clark Little, put on their fins, grab a camera, and head straight on in. Once a big wave surfer himself, he now expresses his talents by taking photographs inside the shorebreak. In less than three years, he has gained international recognition for these mesmeric images, featured on television, in exhibitions and a beautiful new book. 'Its really not that heroic', he laughs. 'My wife wanted a picture of a wave for our bedroom wall. I went out and got a cheap waterproof camera and took some photos thinking I could do it. Some came out great, so I got hooked. With a few camera upgrades and a desire to get the next best shot, there's no going back. Besides, who needs an office when the ocean is just such a great place to be'. Kelly Slater, the nine-time world surfing champion, agrees. 'The sea is our home, but Clark is special, certainly our most mental friend!'

Clark creates a self-portrait within a favourite break on the North Shore, Oahu, the third largest of the Hawaiian Islands and a place famous for big waves. Later that year, just along the coast, the ultimate surfing competition was held. It was only the eighth time, since the event was founded in 1984, that conditions have been right. Known as 'The Eddie' after the legendary surfer and North Shore lifeguard Eddie Aikau, it only happens when the open-ocean swells reach twenty feet in Waimea Bay. The entrants were twenty-eight of the best surfers in the world, including Slater, Bruce Irons and Sunny Garcia. Thousands gathered to watch from the beach. Greg Long emerged, unscathed, as the eventual winner – he rode a monster wave, over thirty foot high, in the final heat. He was lucky to make it out alive.

ATLANTIC OCEAN, 1928
ALAN VILLIERS 1903-1982

Alan Villiers appears with his camera, aloft on the royal yard of *Herzogin Cecilie*. A prolific author and film-maker, Villiers sailed all the world's oceans on square-rigged ships. His elegant writings celebrated the culture of the sea, and his photographs – among the finest ever taken afloat – captured a way of life declining rapidly in the face of technological change. The golden age of sail would soon disappear over the horizon.

Villiers was born in Melbourne in 1903, the second son of an Australian poet. He grew up close to the docks and the years watching merchant vessels enflamed his passion for the great ocean-going ships. He first went to sea as a fifteen-year old apprentice on a barque operating in the Tasman. He learnt quickly, working his way to able seaman rating, earning the respect of his shipmates. Temporarily injured and put ashore, he found work as a journalist in Tasmania. When a Norwegian whaling fleet called in at Hobart he seized the opportunity to join them as a reporter on the first modern whaling expedition to Antarctica. He sent his stories back using the ship's radio and they were sold around the world. His passion for sailing ships, and his talent in writing about them, would define the rest of his life.

In 1927, taking leave from his job as a senior reporter, Villiers joined the German windjammer *Herzogin Cecilie*, and described its thrilling race against the Swedish barque *Beatrice*. His voyage to England gave him material for his first bestseller, *Falmouth for Orders*. He signed on with *Grace Harwar*, the last full-rigger in the Australian trade, and sailed

for England making a documentary in the process. The passage was a harrowing one – his close friend was killed in an accident, the ship was under-provisioned and the crew developed scurvy – but for the public, at least, it was thrilling stuff. Villiers had captured over 6,000 feet of film and his book *By Way of Cape Horn* became a classic.

In 1934, at the age of just thirty-one, he bought his own ship, the *Joseph Conrad* and embarked on a round-the-world voyage with an international crew made up mostly of young cadets eager to learn seamanship. Over the next four years he sailed over 58,000 miles. In 1938 he began an examination of sailing culture in the Far East, spending eighteen months on an Arab dhow sailing to Zanzibar and back. Though the Second World War brought adventures like these to an end, he continued to teach while also assisting in the Allies' sea operations. In peacetime, his career flourished. His writings, photography and lectures made him famous; he sailed movie ships for Hollywood and captained the *Mayflower II* across the Atlantic. 'Looking back', he later joked, on summing up his ocean-going life, 'I am appalled at the amount of almost wild rushing about the earth that I have done in the process of making a living'. However, as a trustee of the National Maritime Museum and in his advocacy and devotion to ship preservation and sail training, Villiers left a profound legacy to the ocean world. His magnificent love affair with the sea produced over forty books, which taken together read as a eulogy in the twilight of commercial sail.

COWES, 2003
SAM DAVIES 1974 -

Sam Davies won international attention as a debutante in the 2008-09 Vendée Globe, where she beat of most of the male competition to finish fourth. Of thirty boats in all, only eleven completed the gruelling race. She was one of the few sailors to cover more than 400 miles in one day. She also diverted her course to go to the aid of fellow competitor, Yann Eliès, who had broken his leg. He was airlifted to safety. Throughout the challenge, her enthusiastic dispatches were a joy for both her fans and her sponsors. She was most recently nominated for the 2009 ISAF World Sailor of the Year Awards.

Portsmouth-born, Davies grew up on Hayling Island with her 'sailing-mad' parents but currently lives and trains in Brittany. She has risen through the ranks to become one of the top offshore racers in the world, with the best record of any of the current female skippers. Her early race experience was as a member of Tracy Edwards' all-female crew in their bid for the Jules Verne Trophy, before their yacht dismasted in the Southern Ocean. She would go on to make the Figaro her speciality, completing four Solitaires in 30-foot Beneteaus, before graduating to larger open-ocean racing boats. She moved to Port-la-Forêt where she has learnt from many of the top French professionals, including the legendary Michel Desjoyeaux. It was not long before she was at the helm of his Open 60, which she renamed *Roxy* after the French clothing company became her major sponsor. In June 2009 Davies teamed up with rival skipper Dee Caffari and an all-female crew to claim the Round Britain and Ireland monohull record, completing the difficult navigation on *Aviva* in just 6 days and 11 hours.

The darling of the press on both sides of the Channel, she has quickly become the most recognisable woman in the world of sailing, perhaps destined to become the most visible of all. 'Sam Davies', runs one commentary, 'is infectiously buoyant, remarkably skilled, and well on her way to achieving rock-star status. She looks like a swimsuit model, sure, but that doesn't change the fact that she's a solid, world-class competitor'. She now has the 2012 Vendée in her sights – all she needs is a new boat.

CHARLESTON, 1864
POWDER MONKEY n.d.

A young sailor leans proudly against his gun on the USS *New Hampshire*, off Charleston, South Carolina. It is 1864 and America is being torn apart by a brutal civil war. The bombardment of the Confederate-held city continues, and it was not until the following February that it finally surrendered to the Union. This portrait was captured by Mathew Brady, one of the most celebrated nineteenth-century photographers, who became famous for his dramatic images from the battlefields of the war. He was a pioneer of a new type of dangerous, investigative photojournalism, despite the huge personal and financial risk: 'I had to go', he later said, 'a spirit in my feet said go, and so I went'. We don't know the name of the young boy he photographed that day, or if the child survived the bloody conflict to come.

In December 1860, following the election of Abraham Lincoln, the South Carolina General Assembly had made the state the first to secede from the Union, and early the following year the first shots of the American Civil War were fired when citadel cadets attacked the Union ship *Star of the West* as she entered Charleston's harbour. After a thirty-four hour bombardment, Union-held Fort Sumter also fell to Confederate control and the city soon became a key centre for operations of their fledgling navy. The Atlantic Ocean port was a safe harbour for the blockade runners, and it was from Charleston in February 1864 that the first attack by submarine, the *H.L. Hunley*, was launched on the USS *Housatonic*.

Children fought in the Civil War, both on land and at sea. This young 'powder monkey', a boy perhaps no more than ten years old, was assigned to keep crews supplied with gunpowder and cannon balls during the mêlée of the fight, a crucial responsibility. During the war, Brady spent over $100,000 to create 10,000 plates. He expected the US government to buy the photographs but when they refused he was forced to sell his studio and file for bankruptcy. Though Congress granted him some funds in 1875, he remained deeply in debt. Depressed by the loss of his eyesight and the death of his wife, Brady passed away in the charity ward of a hospital in New York in 1896. Though he had created some of the most important portraits of his generation, including eighteen American Presidents – his Lincoln is now used on the $5 bill – he died penniless and alone, a hero of photography long forgotten.

DORA, 2009

DON WALSH 1931-

Submarine captain, war veteran and preeminent marine explorer Don Walsh greets us at his home in Dora, Oregon. Tucked in the mountains, it's a fair way from the broad Pacific, but he is surrounded by memories of a lifetime's adventure at sea. After graduation from the US Naval Academy, he saw service in both the Korean and Vietnam wars. Walsh was the Navy's first deep submersible pilot and commanded the bathyscaphe *Trieste* from 1958-1962. For the past forty years he has remained active in the design, construction and operation of deep submersibles.

In 1960, he and Jacques Piccard piloted *Trieste* to the deepest point in the world's oceans; seven miles down in the Mariana Trench, an unbeatable record for which he remains rightly proud. He is also an experienced polar traveller. Having worked at the North and South Poles, he has made over fifty expeditions. Antarctica's 'Walsh Spur', a remote mountain ridge, is named in his honour.

From the dark abyssal depths, to the mighty Southern Ocean, through his courage and vision Walsh rose to the top of his field. In his lectures and books he has shaped our understanding of the seas. He expanded the realm of the possible and for that alone he deserves the description frequently given him: a 'living legend'. Of all the modern figures featured in this book, it is Walsh who has been singled out by his peers. Still energetic, this year thousands of well-wishers will join him in celebrating the fiftieth anniversary of his epic adventure to the 'bottom of the world' in *Trieste*. His advice now, is the same as it always was: 'Embrace life and always act on your curiosity. That's the definition of exploration. There are millions of things yet to be discovered in the World Ocean'. 'Actually', Walsh tells me later, 'I thought President Kennedy said it even better: "We are all tied to the ocean. And when we go back to the sea, whether it is to sail or to watch – we are going back from whence we came"'.

BERMUDA, 1930
OTIS BARTON 1899-1992

Harvard graduate Frederick Otis Barton Jnr was a wealthy adventurer, engineer, combat photographer, author and sometime-actor turned undersea pioneer. His portrait was captured in 1930 as he posed in his 'Barton Tank', the world's first bathysphere, which he had devised and financed to take underwater photographs. Designed by Captain Butler of the Cox and Stephens yard in New York, it was cast as a hollow steel sphere one inch thick. Its three tiny windows were made of fused quartz, it carried a high-pressure cylinder of oxygen, and the 400-pound hatchway was bolted down shut before being lowered over the side of a ship, down into the ocean abyss.

To get the help he needed to make his expedition a reality, Barton enlisted the expertise of famed naturalist and explorer William Beebe. In waters off Bermuda, they began the bathysphere's first manned dive and reached a depth of 800 feet. On 15 August 1934, they made a descent to a depth of more than 3,000 feet, a record that remained unbeaten for fifteen years. They only stopped as their cable was about to run out. Their descriptions of a glowing world of undersea creatures enthralled the public: 'cavalcades of black shrimps, transparent eels, and bizarre fish approached the descending sphere', and when Beebe used his spotlight to see them, they retreated, as mysteriously as they came, deep into the shadows. Below them the ocean disappeared into darkness. There, said Beebe, 'lay a world that looked like the black pit-mouth of hell itself'.

A Hollywood film about their adventure, *Titans of the Deep*, was made and after an interim career shooting movies in Panama and Australia, Barton went on to make other descents, including a new record dive in the Pacific in 1949. On this occasion, he was in constant telephone communication with his surface crew and his running commentary was amplified topside to the press by loudspeakers. 'It makes me dizzy', he began, calling out at 500 feet: 'Now the fireworks are really starting ... There's a creature that looks like a long pipe with a row of lights along it. The tentacles of an octopus just dragged by, showering sparks'. Beyond 1,000 feet, 'The headphones are getting cold'; later, 'I see a barrage of luminescent, spirally shrimp beating against the window', and so on as he went ever further down into the depths. After passing the old record he quipped: 'This is an unbelievable world down here. I wish Dr Beebe were with me. He might know what some of these things are!' At 4,000 feet his lights went out. Listeners above could hear his teeth chattering.

HUNTINGTON BEACH, 2010
GEORGE BASS 1932-

Distinguished Professor Emeritus, Dr George Fletcher Bass, jokes with us on the beach in California. We've rescued him from a nearby conference, a meeting of the world's leading archaeologists. But, it's a beautiful morning and we're all pleased to be by the ocean.

Bass has conducted excavations and surveys, mostly off the Turkish coast, since 1960, developing many underwater techniques that are now standard. He was the first to excavate an ancient shipwreck on the seabed and is rightly considered the 'founding father' of ocean archaeology. He laughs when I mention this title – 'that makes me sound so old, doesn't it! It's funny because when I first saw the sea I was about five. My family had taken me to Myrtle Beach and I hated it so much. I got sand burrs in my bare feet. I resolved to avoid the beach altogether. With my slightly older brother, we then planned a submarine we would build – of wood! Not guessing, of course, that almost thirty years later I would launch the first commercially built research submarine in America, General Dynamic's *Asherah*'.

South Carolina born, Bass obtained a masters in Near Eastern Archaeology from the Johns Hopkins University in 1955, followed by two years at the American School of Classical Studies in Athens. After some time in the US Army, he went on to gain his doctorate in Classical Archaeology from the University of Pennsylvania, where he remained as a faculty member until leaving to found the Institute of Nautical Archaeology, now the world's top organisation for ocean survey and excavation. A prolific educator and author – he has written or edited seven books and over a hundred articles – he was awarded the Archaeological Institute of America's Gold Medal, among many other decorations for his work. I remind him that he was once described by *Time* magazine as 'a kind of underwater Indiana Jones'. He smiles. 'Well then, best we get back to work!'

LONDON, 1857
ISAMBARD KINGDOM BRUNEL 1806-1859

Brunel stands before the massive launching chains of the *Great Eastern* in London's Millwall Dock. Originally called 'Leviathan', she was the largest ship yet built. Such was the scale and ambition of the project, it would take another year to get her into the water and she would not be ready to depart on her maiden voyage until the autumn of 1859. By this time, Brunel was mortally sick with a kidney disease, and he would have a seizure on deck as she left. He lived long enough to receive the devastating news of an explosion in the boiler room as she steamed down the English Channel. A lesser ship would have been ruined, but the *Great Eastern* survived and began her career as a passenger liner. She was later converted, laying the first lasting trans-Atlantic telegraph cable in 1866, a major step in connecting the modern world. It could transmit eight words a minute.

Brunel wrote on the back of his original photograph: 'I asked Mr Lenox (the cable engineer) to stand with me, but he would not, so I alone am hung in chains'. Ironically, Robert Howlett's portrait has since become something of an icon, a vision of Brunel's enterprise. First reproduced as a stereoview, it was released as a collectible print, before reincarnating on souvenir china plates, as statues and wax sculptures, and more recently on an endless number of ties, tea towels and t-shirts. It is, without doubt, the most famous image of a man who was a legend in his day, and who remains one of the most remarkable engineers the world has seen. In a BBC poll in 2002, Brunel was voted one of the 'Greatest Britons' ever, narrowly beaten into second place by Winston Churchill. Nonetheless, he left ocean heroes such as Captain Cook, Sir Francis Drake, even Admiral Nelson, trailing in his wake. Not bad for a man who was half French and who had learnt many of his engineering skills across the Channel.

Though his mother was English, his father was the great French engineer Sir Marc Isambard Brunel. Young Brunel was sent oversees for schooling and later studied as an engineer at college in Caen and the Lycée Henri-Quatre in Paris. He was apprenticed to his father who was building a tunnel under the River Thames, before taking up a job to design and build the suspension bridge across the Avon at Clifton – the longest bridge in the world when it was finally completed in 1864. His work in Bristol introduced him to a circle of wealthy merchants, so that in March 1833, when still not quite twenty-seven, he was appointed engineer to the Great Western Railway. For the next fifteen years he devoted much of his phenomenal energy and talent into what became one of the 'finest works in England'. Brunel proposed the line be extended to New York by way of an ocean-going ship operating out of Bristol, and he was duly commissioned with the task of designing and building it. Confounding the critics, Brunel's vast new paddle steamer, the SS *Great Western* completed her maiden voyage to New York in 1838, and his reputation soared. The radical propeller-driven SS *Great Britain* followed her across the Atlantic in 1845, while Brunel set his sights on the third, and the mightiest, of his ships, the SS *Great Eastern*.

SANTA BARBARA, 2010
CONNIE LYN MORGAN 1956-

At dawn on the historic Stearns Wharf, Connie Lyn Morgan greets us before heading out for a dive. California-born, the ocean has always been part of her life. Her father, Bev, opened one of the first dive shops in the state – Dive N' Surf – and was instrumental in the creation of diving certification programs. For over forty years she has worked in the sea, first as a tour guide, to her present position as President of Kirby Morgan Dive Systems, manufacturer of the world-renowned deep-sea commercial diving helmets and masks.

In 2000, she was honoured into the Women Divers Hall of Fame. It's an achievement she modestly enjoys but the most satisfying thing for Connie is that she has been able to do what she loves almost every day of the year. 'Each day is a joy when you are by the sea', she tells me. 'It can be calming, it can be invigorating. It can make your heart burst with happiness while at other times it can terrify you. I think I now have salt water running through my veins. I need to immerse myself regularly. The ocean is life itself!'

GOSPORT, 1954
PETER HAMMERSLEY 1928-

Submarine Lieutenant Peter Hammersley demonstrates his 'advanced escape equipment' in 1954. He was photographed by a press reporter during the Navy's first public demonstration of this radical kit. HMS *Alaric* was an Amphion-class diesel-electric submarine, built by the famous English shipbuilders Cammell Laird. She was designed for action in the deep waters of the Pacific. Vessels of all kinds came from the Cammell Laird yards – the world's first steel ship, the *Ma Roberts* built in 1858 for David Livingstone's expedition up the Zambezi, and the huge ocean liner RMS *Mauretania*, the first built for the Cunard White Star Company.

In response to the start of the Cold War in the early 1950s, the A-class subs were modified for action against Soviet submarines, rather than surface ships. But when *Affray* went missing at sea in 1951 with the loss of seventy-five men, many of the subs were confined in port. The Navy tasked its team of inventors to devise new ways of improving the survival chances of their men. The new system, 'the Free Ascent Method', required the plucky submariner equipped only with goggles, nose clip and inflated life jacket, to reach the surface in a single, deep breath, discharging air from his lungs on his way up. Trainees were put through their paces in the deep testing tank at HMS *Dolphin*. 'The best way to safely remove air is to whistle on the way up', one officer explained, though some wondered if 'crossing their fingers, or praying, might provide a more effective source of assistance'.

Hammersley would go on to serve in Britain's first nuclear submarine HMS *Dreadnought*. He became Captain of the Royal Naval Engineering College at Manadon and later Chief Engineering Officer of the Fleet. In a notable addition to this distinguished career, Rear Admiral 'Spam' Hammersley was also President of the Royal Naval Engineers Quart Club, a beer-drinking society founded to discourage the 'gin habit' in the 1930s. It is now a charitable social group with over 1,200 members worldwide. On his stepping down as President, Hammersley remarked it had been a pleasure to 'quaff some ales' with like-minded fellows. The minutes of the Annual Meeting in 2002, held at the Wheelwrights Arms in Havant, are typical: 'We never finished all the barrels and decided it best to end the meeting as the dancers were getting tired'.

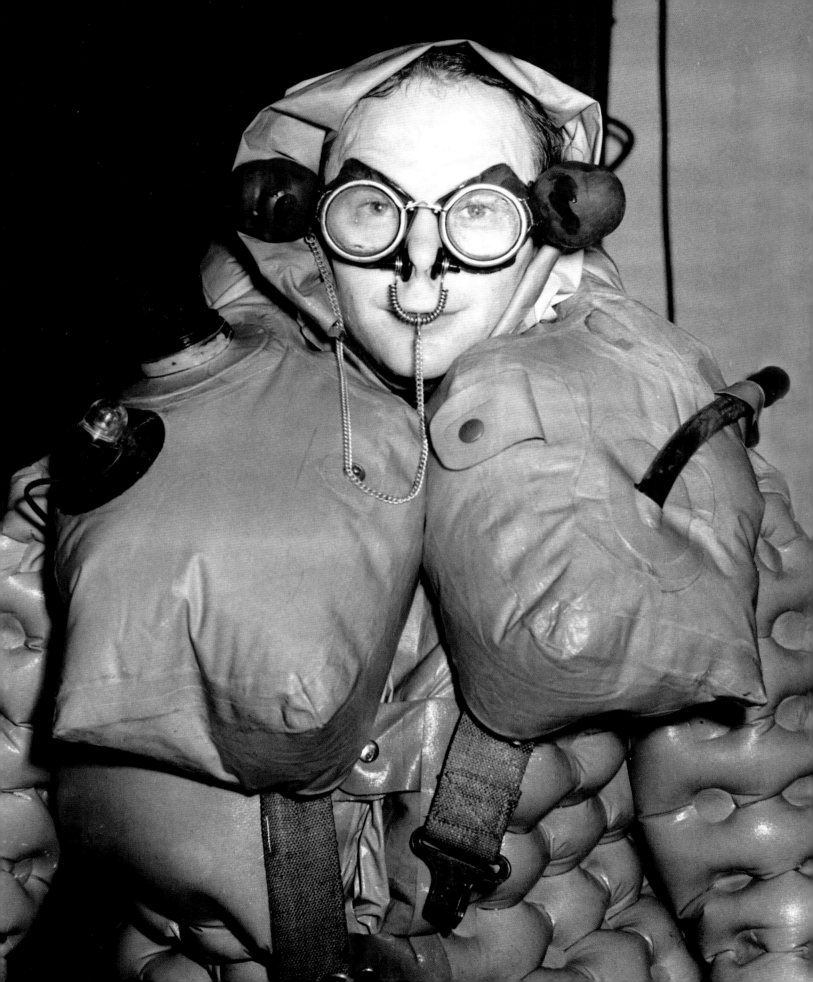

BAHAMAS, 2006
TANYA STREETER 1973-

Reef sharks circle Tanya Streeter in the warm waters of the Bahamas. They are inquisitive, but not threatening. She is filming a documentary for the BBC, *Shark Therapy*, while learning to overcome her fears – the hard way. This world champion freediver, environmentalist and television presenter, is now a proud mother. It will be a while before she does this again.

Born in the Cayman Islands, the sea has always been a part of her life. She took up freediving when she was twenty-five and went on to conquer the new extreme sport. In 2002 she broke both the women's and the men's 'no limit' record – with just a single breath, diving to 525 feet, before manually inflating a liftbag that pulled her back up to the surface. Though some sceptics called her mad, it was a phenomenal act of endurance, which pushed the boundaries of human potential.

Having now retired from the sport, it is her advocacy work, in helping people to understand the importance and fragility of the oceans, of which Streeter is most proud. 'Well, my ongoing project actually is my daughter Tilly', she tells me, 'and hopefully my next project will be a brother or sister for her! Meantime, I'm also involved in developing an animated version of myself for a future kids' television series. That's all well and good, but the most important thing of all is for children to be able to get into the outdoors. We need to give them the chance to become champions for nature themselves. Millions of kids will grow up never seeing the sea. That breaks my heart'.

NEW YORK, 1947
SHERMAN HOYT 1880-1961

Veteran yachtsman C. Sherman Hoyt, who spent more than sixty years on the water, is shown in the model room of his beloved New York Yacht Club. He raced in innumerable classes, from dinghies to America's Cup defenders. A bachelor and naval architect, who usually avoided the limelight, he was persuaded to appear in a *Life* magazine special feature on the joys of sailing in Long Island Sound. This fine portrait was created by Nina Leen, one of the journal's first female photographers.

On 20 September 1934, the New York Yacht Club found themselves in an unusual position. They were losing the America's Cup. After eighty-three years of holding the famous 'Auld Mug', their entry, Harold Vanderbilt's *Rainbow*, was two races down to T.O.M. Sopwith's *Endeavour*, in a best-of-nine series with race three well underway and trailing by almost six minutes. Believing all was lost, Vanderbilt gave up the helm and headed below for coffee and sandwiches. But, in a stroke of genius – some may say fortune – he handed control to afterguard member Sherman Hoyt, whose uncanny ability in light wind was to turn the race in their favour. He outfoxed Sopwith on the downwind leg, sailing right around his opponent. *Rainbow* crossed the finish line with a lead of more than three minutes, turning the tide in America's favour. They went on to win the next three races and in doing so retained the Cup for the Club.

Hoyt is intimately connected with another of the most famous sailing trophies in the world. In 1907 he was victorious at the Tri-Centenary Regatta at Jamestown, Virginia – commemorating the 300th Anniversary of the first permanent settlement in America – and King Edward VII presented him with the winner's trophy. After some time, Hoyt decided to give it to the Royal Bermuda Yacht Club, and proposed a regular one-on-one match series in identical 6-metre yachts. It was an inspired decision. Now, the Bermuda classic is the oldest match racing competition in the world for one-design yachts. Hoyt's vision of a regatta event with a level playing field, would later become the blueprint for other racing events the world over.

The first winner of the Cup in its new format was Briggs Cunningham, who was also the first skipper to win the America's Cup in a 12-metre class boat. The 'King Edward VII Gold Cup' is now a much-coveted prize of the World Match Racing Tour, the jewel in the crown of the International Sailing Federation world championship. The most recent man to lift Hoyt's historic prize, in 2009, was the pre-eminent British sailor Ben Ainslie.

BREST, 1994
SIR PETER BLAKE 1948-2001

Peter Blake is a happy man as thousands cheer him on his return to port in Brittany. As skipper of *Enza*, with his friend Robin Knox-Johnston, he had just circumnavigated the world. In just 74 days and 22 hours, they had also become the fastest men to do it, winning the coveted Jules Verne Trophy in the process. They had just battled through a brutal Atlantic storm, trailing anchor chain to stop their catamaran from pitchpoling. Blake later described it as 'the worst 24 hours' of his life. Photographs of their triumph sped round the globe. The following year, both men were knighted by the Queen for their efforts.

Charismatic New Zealander Blake was a man born for the sea and his achievements are without equal. He competed in five Whitbreads and in his last, in 1990, he skippered the 84-foot ketch *Steinlager 2* to an unprecedented clean sweep, with line, handicap and overall honours on each of the race's six legs. He led his country to successive victories in the America's Cup, the first non-American team to successfully defend this most prestigious sailing prize. In 1997, Blake became the Cousteau Society's head of expeditions and skipper of the schooner *Antarctic Explorer*, which he later bought and renamed *Seamaster*. Soon afterward he was made special envoy for the UN Environment Programme and he began making plans for a number of voyages monitoring ocean pollution and the impacts of global warming.

On 6 December 2001, *Seamaster* was anchored at the mouth of the Amazon when she was boarded at night by a gang of masked pirates. Blake was shot in the back as he rushed to help his crew and died shortly afterwards. In a moment of senseless barbarity, the world had lost not only one of its finest sailors but also a great man. Blake is buried at Warblington churchyard, near Emsworth on the south coast of England, where he had settled with his wife Pippa and their two children. His headstone bears the words of John Masefield's poem *Sea Fever*: 'I must down to the sea again, to the lonely sea and the sky, and all I ask is a tall ship and a star to steer her by...'

NEW YORK, 1962
SIR FRANCIS CHICHESTER 1901-1972

Francis Charles Chichester, celebrated navigator and sailor, was born in Devon but later emigrated to New Zealand with only ten sovereigns in his pocket. He tried a variety of jobs, before finding success as a property developer, earning a substantial income. He bought a plane, a de Havilland Gipsy Moth, and learnt to fly at a New Zealand Air Force base. In 1929 he set off from England to Australia and after nineteen days' solo flight landed in Sydney to a rapturous welcome. He was the second person ever to complete this dangerous trip. In 1931 he determined to become the first to fly solo across the Tasman Sea. He navigated in his small cockpit with just a sextant, logarithmic tables, and a scribbling pad strapped to his knee. He made two landings en route, one on the tiny Lord Howe Island where his plane sank and had to be rebuilt before he could fly to safety. After reaching Australia he made the first solo flight to Japan on what he hoped would be the first leg of an epic round-the-world expedition, but he later crashed into telephone wires, seriously injuring himself and writing off his plane.

After leaving hospital, he took up ocean racing, first as a navigator and later, in 1958, with his own boat, *Gipsy Moth II*. The following year he was diagnosed with lung cancer and told he had just six months to live, but he recovered sufficiently to win the first single-handed trans-Atlantic race. This candid portrait at the Minneford Yacht Yard, New York, shows Chichester gathering in a sail at the bow of his *Gipsy Moth III*, after the finish of his record-breaking second solo trip across the Atlantic. In 1966 he began his greatest adventure, departing Plymouth in his ketch *Gipsy Moth IV*, to sail alone around the world, stopping only once in Australia. After 226 days of sailing, a crowd of more than 250,000 people were waiting at the harbour to welcome him home. 'I told myself for a long time that anyone who tried to round the Horn in a small yacht must be crazy', he later wrote, 'but for years it was in the back of my mind. It not only scared me, frightened me, but I think it would be fair to say that it terrified me'.

Chichester's hero Joshua Slocum had completed the first solo circumnavigation in 1898, but it had taken him three years and numerous stops. Chichester's first words on stepping back on dry land were characteristic: 'What I would like after four months of my own cooking is the best dinner from the best chef in the best surroundings and in the best company'. He would soon be celebrated at gala dinners all over the world. When Chichester was honoured by the Queen in 1967 she used the same sword Queen Elizabeth I had used when knighting Francis Drake, the first Englishman to complete a circumnavigation.

Chichester finally succumbed to cancer in 1972. *Gipsy Moth IV* was for some time on display in Greenwich, land-locked in dry dock next to the famous clipper *Cutty Sark*. Rescued from neglect and restored, she is now based in Cowes, where she is used as a training yacht for young people. During his lifetime Chichester had been fairly honest about his feelings for her: 'Now that I have finished, I don't know what will become of *Gipsy Moth IV*. I only own the stern while my cousin owns two thirds. My part, I would sell any day. It would be better if about a third were sawn off. *Gipsy Moth IV* has no sentimental value for me at all. She is cantankerous and difficult and needs a crew of three – a man to navigate, an elephant to move the tiller and a chimpanzee with arms 8-feet long to get about below and work some of the gear'.

PORT-LA-FORÊT, 2008
MICHEL DESJOYEAUX 1965-

Michel Desjoyeaux is one of the world's best solo sailors, if not the greatest. For more than twenty-five years he has dominated inshore and offshore racing, from full-crewed to solo navigations, from bowman to skipper, on mono and multihulls, small and large. He has made over twenty Atlantic crossings and has raced three times round the world. It's usually fairly easy to get sailors to talk about their accomplishments, but Desjoyeaux doesn't rest on his laurels, and he doesn't care much for reciting the past. To him, 'experience is something you wear on your back, so that you don't ever have to look at it'. His portrait comes as he was training aboard *Foncia*, shortly before the start of the Vendée Globe Race.

His Vendée campaign was not an easy one. He sailed 200 miles before having to return to port with electrical problems. He rejoined the race two days later, although by now almost 400 miles behind the leaders. With intelligent tactics and cool persistence, one after another he gradually overtook his competitors and eventually took the lead off the coast of Australia. He did not look back. The international sailing community was thrilled by his endeavours. When he returned to France in February 2009, after 84 days 3 hours and 9 minutes at sea – a new race record – he was overwhelmed by a crowd of thousands. When he stepped back on dry land he was typically understated: 'for sure I appreciate this sailing trip. I had a nice voyage. It was hard sometimes, but not as hard as last time. When you appreciate what you do it's not difficult, it's a pleasure'.

For a man who has achieved so much in the sport, his modesty and enthusiasm for life is refreshing. 'No goals, I just take opportunities', he says. 'I have no career plans to follow race after race, new boats after new boats. I don't manage my life like that – I just go forward, I stay playful and I respect the ocean. I do it because I love sailing, nothing else. But, I am always learning things that surprise me, so that makes it easy to surprise others! You can't be a copy machine, just making reproductions of your accomplishments – every day should be surprising'.

LONDON, 1866
SIR LEWIS JONES 1797-1895

The 'grand old man' of the British Navy, Vice Admiral Sir Lewis Jones shifts impatiently under the photographer's gaze. This recently-discovered portrait was taken by the London duo Elliot and Fry, in their stylish Baker Street studios. Doubtless, Lewis wouldn't have given a fig for fashion but perhaps decided to have a quick portrait taken as a memento for his family. He had just been promoted.

Born in County Sligo on Christmas Eve, 1797, Lewis Tobias Jones was the third of eleven children. He entered the Navy on New Year's Day 1808, just a week after his eleventh birthday. In 1816 he was midshipman in the *Granicus* at the Bombardment of Algiers and then saw service in the North Sea, the West Indies and Newfoundland. He was on *Princess Charlotte*, the flagship of Sir Robert Stopford, in actions off the coast of Syria in 1840. He later had command of *Sampson* and distinguished himself in the anti-slavery cruises, including the destruction of slave barracoons at Lagos in 1851, a bloody action in which he was commended for 'gallantry, firmness, judgment and energy'. Still in *Sampson*, he was senior officer at the Bombardment of Odessa and continued on operations in the Black Sea throughout the Crimean War. In 1859, with his flag in *Impérieuse* as Rear Admiral of the Blue, he distinguished himself both in blowing things up and getting wounded. He commanded the gunboats at the storming of the Taku Forts during the Second Opium War. From 1884 he was Governor of Greenwich Hospital, then a new training college for officers, where the veteran was fondly admired for his lively humour and straightforward good sense.

Jones sat for this portrait sometime in 1866. As a newly promoted vice admiral, with the two eight-pointed stars dominant on his shoulder epaulettes, his dress uniform is awash with medals. Most prominent on his chest is the star of the Most Honourable Order of the Bath; its riband sash, a swathe of crimson red, crosses his body. Next to it is the distinctive pouched red ribbon of the *Legion d'honneur*, the highest decoration of France, established by that old foe of the Royal Navy, Napoleon, back in 1802. Its badge is a Maltese star, enamelled white with a laurel and oak wreath between its five arms. Around Jones' neck is the star of the Order of the Medjidie, awarded by Sultan Abd-ul-Mejid for assisting the Ottoman Empire during the Crimean War. Its red and green ribbon lies hidden beneath his luxuriant beard.

In 1894, at the age of ninety-seven, Jones earned the honour of 'grand old man' of the Navy, the oldest living British officer, after the centenarian Admiral of the Fleet Provo Wallace passed away. Newspapers in America celebrated his achievement. Though remembered now, if at all, for his longevity, Jones' naval career was an explosive one that saw him serve in most of the major Victorian actions. His 'zeal, bravery, and professionalism' brought him well-deserved success on seas across the globe. In 1895, after being confined to bed for two days at his sister's home in Southsea, the old Admiral departed on his final voyage.

ENGLISH CHANNEL, 2009
MIKE BOYCE 1943-

Mike Boyce joins the crew of a lifeboat for sea trials off Poole one winter afternoon late in December. Until his retirement from active duty, Admiral the Lord Boyce GCB OBE DL, to use his full title, was the most senior officer in the Royal Navy. He now directs his talent and passion for the ocean as an active supporter of a range of maritime organisations. He is especially pleased to be Chairman of the Royal National Lifeboat Institution, the charity dedicated to saving lives at sea.

Born in Cape Town, Boyce joined the Royal Navy in 1961. He qualified as a submariner and had a range of commands, including a nuclear attack submarine, at the cutting-edge of the Cold War. Among other duties, he commanded the frigate HMS *Brilliant* and had the role of Senior Naval Officer Middle East. He was promoted to the Flag List in 1991 and was subsequently Flag Officer Sea Training; Flag Officer Surface Flotilla; Commander-in-Chief Naval Home Command and Commander-in-Chief Fleet, the admiral responsible for the operation, resourcing and training of all the ships, submarines, aircraft and personnel in the Navy. During this period he was knighted and held a variety of senior NATO commands. He became First Sea Lord in 1998 and later Chief of the Defence Staff, before taking a well-earned retirement from the service in 2003.

He was elevated to the peerage as Baron Boyce and was appointed Lord Warden and Admiral of the Cinque Ports in 2004, one of the highest honours bestowed by the Sovereign. As well as his work for the RNLI, Boyce is a Trustee of the National Maritime Museum and a Patron of the Tall Ships Youth Trust, the Submariners' Association and Sail 4 Cancer, among many other worthwhile causes. 'The ocean is inspirational', he explains, 'because of its huge variability and unpredictability. It's our lifeline, it decides our climate, it's a place for adventure yet it still contains great mystery. At sea you can experience the full spectrum of sense and emotion: colour, sound, smell, touch, fear, love, hatred, and joy. And it desperately needs our help because simply not enough people understand that its health is crucial to our shared future'.

CROMER, 1942
HENRY BLOGG 1876-1954

Henry George Blogg is the RNLI's most decorated lifeboatman. He was Coxswain at the Norfolk station for almost forty years and during his fifty-three years of service was awarded three Gold and four Silver Medals for Gallantry. Fierce northeasterly gales would push the waters of the North Sea onto the north Norfolk coast, making a perilous lee shore for shipping. Known as the 'Devil's Throat', for centuries this coastline was littered with shipwrecks. Blogg's crew launched a total of 387 times, helping save some 873 lives. Blogg was, in the words of his contemporaries, 'one of the bravest men who ever lived'. Surprisingly, he never learnt to swim.

Blogg was thrust into public attention, following his rescue of eleven sailors from the Swedish steamer *Fernebo* during the terrible winter of 1917. His ageing crew had already been rowing in mountainous seas for several hours, rescuing sixteen men from the Greek ship *Pyrin*. It was not until midnight, under the light of searchlights from the cliff-top, that Blogg's boat was able to plough through the breakers to reach the second vessel and take off its crew. He won the first of his Gold Medals for his courage on this occasion. His second was for saving fifteen men from the Dutch tanker *Georgia*, an epic rescue that took more than twenty hours at sea. His third came in 1941, for saving forty-four men from a merchant steamer off Hammond's Knoll sandbank, in gale-force seas and under aerial attack from a German bomber. Hit at the helm of his motor lifeboat by a monster wave, and knocked overboard, Blogg would have drowned but for being hauled up from the raging torrent by his men.

Despite public fame, Blogg remained a modest man who neither smoked nor drank. He had a quiet kindness that endeared him to everyone he met and, most important of all, he inspired confidence in his crew: 'quick and resolute in decision, unerring in judgement, fearless before danger'. Blogg lived in Cromer all his life, working as a crab fisherman and letting out deckchairs and beach huts, with his faithful dog Monte at his side. He stood down in 1947, at the age of seventy-one, eleven years past the usual retirement age. The following year, the new Cromer lifeboat was named the *Henry Blogg* in his honour and his nephew, Henry 'Shrimp' Davies, took over as its coxswain. Blogg said it was the happiest day of his life.

ANAMBAS ISLANDS, 2009
WALLACE NICHOLS 1967-

Dr Wallace J. Nichols is a leading sea turtle researcher and ocean advocate. He's a Research Associate at the California Academy of Sciences, founder of Ocean Revolution and a past-president of the International Sea Turtle Society, but he wears his academic knowledge lightly. For over a decade he has been working along the Pacific coast of Baja California Sur and in archipelagos off Indonesia, where this portrait was taken. With collaborative efforts from local fishermen and other non-profits, his work is informing new conservation strategies. 'Sea turtles are sentinels for the ocean', he says. 'They're my portal into everything'.

He is one of a new generation of ocean champions – trained in the sciences and Internet savvy – who are able to use the strength of their research and the reach of new media to really make a difference. He is an ardent international spokesman for turtle conservation, appearing on television programs such as *PBS Nature*, *National Geographic Explorer* and *Animal Planet* as well as documentary films including Leonardo DiCaprio's *The 11th Hour* and *Beautiful Wave*. His commitment to the sea has become a guiding passion: 'When one understands its role and enormity, it's impossible to overstate the significance of the ocean to all of us'.

LONDON, 1876
SAMUEL PLIMSOLL 1824-1898

A Bristol-born statesman and social reformer, Samuel Plimsoll began his career as a coal merchant in London where his research into the trade made him aware of the dangers that sailors faced. When his father died, Plimsoll was left to support his mother and five young children. In 1868 he was elected as the Liberal Member of Parliament for Derby, and struggled in vain for many years campaigning against the 'coffin ships'; unseaworthy and ill-equipped vessels, often heavily insured, in which unscrupulous ship owners risked the lives of their crews. A few years previously, for example, when the emigrant ship *London* sailed down the Thames bound for Australia, she carried 220 passengers, 69 crew, her holds and decks over-laden with cargo. A seaman watching her pass Purfleet said, 'It'll be her last voyage ... she's too low down in the water, she'll never rise to a stiff sea'. He was right. She sank in the Bay of Biscay. There were only 19 survivors.

Dubbed 'the Sailors Friend' in the press, Plimsoll continued to lobby Parliament. His speeches in the House caused controversy; at one stage he was forcibly removed after railing at his opponents and calling greedy ship owners 'villains' and 'mercenary scoundrels'. The hacks of *Vanity Fair* delighted in his 'crusading madness': 'He is not a clever man, he is a poor speaker and a feeble writer, but he has a big good heart, and with the untutored utterings of that he has stirred even the most indifferent'. With a wave of public support behind him, he finally persuaded Parliament to amend the 1871 Merchant Shipping Act. It ensured that a 'Plimsoll Line', marked on a ship's side, was a legal requirement – the line would disappear below water if a ship were dangerously overloaded. This portrait was captured in 1876 by the society photographers Samuel Lock and George Whitfield at their fashionable London studio, the same year Plimsoll's line was first applied.

In recognition of his efforts, the RNLI presented him with a silver model lifeboat and named a new boat in his honour, launched in Christmas that year. Plimsoll retired from public life to Kent, having lost an eye and left physically worn out by his work. By the time of his death in 1898, Plimsoll's reforming had also ruined him financially. All the ships in Folkestone harbour had their flags at half-mast and a contingent of sailors drew his hearse and shouldered his body for burial, in tribute to the man who had devoted his life to campaign on their behalf.

ARDMORE, 2009
JOHN RIDGWAY 1938-

We join veteran yachtsman John Ridgway at his remote home in Ardmore, nestled on the Scottish hillside above the loch. At the foot of the croft, the sea greets us. 'It's a magic carpet', he smiles, 'one that has carried me three times round the planet and so much more besides'. His expeditions have taken him down the Amazon, among the treacherous ice of Antarctica, through the Spanish Sahara, the Himalayas and the Peruvian Andes, but without doubt, he tells us, it's the freedom of the ocean that has proven the defining feature of his life.

Tough and supremely capable, Ridgway is perhaps best known in Britain for his heroics in 1966, with Chay Blyth, when they became the second pair to row the Atlantic. They had an open wooden dory not a world away from that used by the Norwegian-born seamen George Harbo and Frank Samuelsen, who had dared the crossing in 1896. Ridgway and Blyth carried 120 gallons of water and 80 days' worth of dehydrated curry, a third of which was spoiled by seawater. More or less out of touch from the world for 91 days, they were 'told of England's World Cup victory over scrambled eggs on board a tanker bound for Venezuela that stopped to help them out'. When they made landfall on the Aran Islands, off the west coast of Ireland, and saw its green grass, Ridgway remembers it as one of the happiest moments in his life.

In 2003, Ridgway and his wife Marie Christine, his companion on many of his adventures, embarked on one final voyage around the world, to raise awareness for a wonderful cause – the protection of that most noble of seabirds, the albatross. 'We paid for this one entirely ourselves. It was something we felt we just had to do and we looked for nothing in return. We simply took our petition to the United Nations and sailed back to Ardmore, our home for these past forty-five years. Now seventy-one, I sometimes feel a little like Greta Garbo: *I want to be alone!* After seeing the albatross in the Southern Ocean over six decades, I'm rather hoping to become one when I die'.

SOUTHAMPTON, 1949
DONALD SORRELL 1894-1958

Captain Donald Sorrell braves the media glare at a press call one cold January morning in Southampton, just before his ship *Caronia* made her maiden voyage to New York. Known as the 'Green Goddess' for her distinctive livery, she was the first ship ever purpose-built for the dual role of passenger crossings and luxury cruising. With her fabulous art-deco interiors and high crew to passenger ratio, she quickly became the post-war jewel of the British Merchant Navy, with a Cunard career spanning nearly twenty years. Sorrell served as RMS *Caronia*'s captain through to 1951, making over thirty Atlantic crossings in addition to a great number of cruises in the West Indies.

Born in London, Sorrell went to sea at the age of fifteen aboard the square-rigger *William Mitchell*, as the first in his family to try a life at sea. During the four years of his apprenticeship he ferried coal to Chile, joined a voyage to Australia, and made a final run to the South Pacific in the barque *Falkirk*. In 1914, as third officer of the British India Steam Navigation Company's *Urlana*, he helped to transport a Sikh regiment from Bombay to Marseilles in the first convoy of the First World War. Two years later, in Hong Kong, Captain Sorrell acquired his master's ticket.

He joined the Cunard Steamship Company in 1918 and during the next two decades served on a score of grand ocean liners, including *Mauretania*, the world's fastest, and the beautiful old four-stacked *Aquitania*. He was chief officer of RMS *Georgic* when she went to Norway in June 1940 to evacuate British, French and Polish troops. The ship took out some 3,000 men while Nazi planes hunted them. Ten days later he was ordered to take part in a similar evacuation at Saint-Nazaire. He and his crew brought 5,000 British soldiers out of France while under constant air attack.

In 1953, Sorrell attracted the attention of the newspapers for docking the 81,000-ton *Queen Mary* – the size of the Empire State Building – without the usual fleet of tugboats, owing to a strike in New York. His use of an ebb tide, winches, a rowboat and a small motor launch, was heralded as 'a feat of seamanship among seamen'. He retired in 1956 and died peacefully at home shortly afterwards. An obituary in *The New York Times* described this veteran of ocean cruising: 'A short, slender, soft-spoken man, of ruddy complexion, Captain Sorrell was one of the ablest Cunard masters. In his forty-seven year career at sea he had climbed the ratlines and swung the capstan bars of square-riggers and had navigated the largest ocean liners'.

MANDELLO DEL LARIO, 2009

ALEX BELLINI 1978-

Italian adventurer Alexandro Bellini first attempted to row the Atlantic in 2004, before technical problems and bad weather forced his boat onto the rocks of Formentera Island, off the coast of Spain. In 2005, after 226 days and almost 10,000 miles at sea, he finally reached Brazil. Despite the hardship of this solo voyage, the ocean had Bellini in its thrall. His thoughts quickly turned to the biggest challenge of them all – the Pacific.

In 2008, after ten months of rowing and drifting some 9,500 nautical miles alone across the ocean, Bellini was forced to end his voyage just sixty-five miles short of Australia. Exhausted, severely malnourished and with poor weather approaching, he called for help by satellite phone. He was tantalizingly close, and it must have been a heart-breaking decision to take. This charismatic portrait was captured by Andrea Raso after Bellini had returned home to safety. Asked why her husband did it, Francesca Bellini told newspapers, 'He is an extreme sportsman, he's not after records'. It was an inward journey to discover something of himself, Bellini tells me. At the mercy of the open ocean he had found his answer. He has now promised his wife he would not dare try it again.

The Atlantic was first crossed in an open boat by a pair of Norwegian-American immigrants in 1896. Frank Samuelsen, a merchant sailor and George Harbo, a surfboat fisherman, had risked their lives for the promise of prize money. They are largely forgotten today. The great ocean would not be dared again until 1966, when the soldiers John Ridgway and Chay Blyth rowed for 92 days in a 20-foot wooden dory. Since then, the once perilous voyage has become an attractive adventure sport – hundreds have followed them and many more have tried, but failed, to make it across. Ridgway's motivation was simple: 'I was trying to make my name,' he said afterwards. 'That's why I was doing it. That's what ambitious people do'. Blyth was equally direct. Like adventurers throughout history, he wanted to find escape. 'It didn't really matter what it was', he explained sometime later, 'I was keen to have a go'. Blyth's only experience of the sea before taking on the open ocean was a short trip on a cross-Channel ferry. For Bellini, struggling against the ocean has enabled him to explore a new mental territory. But for now, he's enjoying a new passion – hot air ballooning.

LOWESTOFT, 1895
FISHERMAN n.d.

This remarkable portrait was taken by George Davison, renowned pictorial photographer, political activist and patron of the arts. Son of a Sunderland shipwright, young Davison was born in the Suffolk village where he returned to create some of his finest work. On the edge of the North Sea, Lowestoft is the most easterly town in the United Kingdom and for centuries was just a small fishing and farming village perched on the cliff-top. But, after its harbour was developed in the 1830s, the town's fortunes improved rapidly. Regular steamers would travel to and from London, a railway connection was added in 1847, and business and tourists soon followed. Trade links were established with Norway and Denmark and seaside hotels, taverns, and shipyards supported a thriving economy. At its peak, in the early twentieth century, there were as many as a thousand sailing boats in the port alone. Its most lucrative export was herring, known locally as the 'silver darling', and workers came from all over the country to help with the catch.

Davison was an elected council member of the Royal Photographic Society, and became deeply involved in artistic debates about the future of the art. In time he resigned from the society and he, with ten others, formed a bohemian brotherhood that later became the renowned photographers' collective, the 'Linked Ring'. The turning point in his career, however, came in 1889 when George Eastman – impressed with his photographic talent and organizing skills – appointed him director of the British branch of his Photographic Materials Company. In 1897, he became assistant manager of the growing business, renamed 'Kodak Limited'. Though his salary was modest, after some savvy decisions he became one of the company's leading shareholders, second only to Eastman himself. By the time Eastman asked him to resign in 1912, Davison was an anarchic millionaire who had all but given up photography.

COMOROS ISLANDS, 2009
JON BOWERMASTER 1954-

Jon Bowermaster takes a break in the warm waters of the Indian Ocean. A six-time grantee of the National Geographic Expeditions Council and an award-winning writer and film-maker, he recently concluded his OCEANS 8 project. It was an ambitious ten-year global expedition that took him around the world by sea kayak, down the coast of Vietnam, into the heart of the Aleutian Islands, within the Tuamotu Atolls of French Polynesia and amongst towering icebergs off the Antarctic Peninsula. From magazine articles through to educational curricula, the lively dispatches from his travels have now travelled the globe.

Seeing the world from the seat of a kayak has given Bowermaster a one-of-a-kind perspective to consider both the health of the planet's waters and the lives of the nearly three billion people around the globe who depend on them. His website and daily blog, *Notes from Sea Level*, draw attention to the latest concerns. His companion book to the DisneyNature film *Oceans* was launched at its premiere on Earth Day in 2010. 'People go to the edge of the sea for a variety of reasons', he tells me. 'The rich go for respite, the poor to find work, holiday-seekers for relaxation. Just sitting at the ocean's edge looking toward the horizon line where blue-meets-blue is revitalizing and chastening for me. The ocean is life itself but it needs our help'.

HALIFAX, 1944
HENRY LARSEN 1899-1964

It's a sunny morning in Nova Scotia in July 1944. Canadian-Norwegian explorer Henry Larsen poses for his portrait on the deck of his wooden motor schooner, *St Roch*. In 1950, she chugged back into Halifax harbour having completed the first circumnavigation of North America via the Panama Canal. Though the pioneering voyage took just 137 sailing days, Larsen had spent the best part of five years ferrying supplies to remote outposts throughout the labyrinthine waterways of northern Canada. As an exercise in asserting sovereignty over a barren, largely unexplored region of some half a million square miles, it was a huge public success, but equally what seemed to many like a futile exercise. But, in the geopolitical scramble in the North, then as now, gestures are all important.

Henry Asbjörn Larsen was born in Norway and began his sea career as an apprentice in the fisheries. He graduated from the Norwegian State Navigation School, did his duty with a six-month stretch in the Norwegian Navy and then signed on as mate on the steamer *Roosevelt*. By 1924 he was mate of the schooner *Maid of Orleans* and made a number of trading voyages to the Arctic. He moved to Canada in 1927, becoming a British citizen. The following year he joined the Royal Canadian Mounted Police, though he later confessed to never having ridden a horse before.

Larsen had timed his entry perfectly. They were building their own patrol ship, *St Roch*, and he was the ideal man to lead her. One of the last wooden ships to operate in the Arctic, her round bottom, designed to escape ice pressure, sent her bucking and heaving in a gale 'like a bronco'. Larsen called her the 'Ugly Duckling' and declared her the most uncomfortable ship he had ever been in. *St Roch* had other honours. Between June 1940 and October 1942 she sailed from Vancouver to Halifax, becoming the first vessel to traverse the Passage from west to east. Larsen's dedication to Arctic work was unswerving. Over an eight-year period he took only one short trip south, he recalled, 'to get married and learn to walk again with ordinary shoes'.

Larsen was promoted to staff sergeant after the first crossing, commissioned with the rank of inspector after the second, and later made a superintendent. He remained with the 'Mounties' until his retirement in 1961, when he moved with his family to Vancouver. He was the author of five books and his autobiography, *The Big Ship*, was published in 1967, a few years after his death. One of his final remarks, written in a letter to a friend, was that he would 'soon be setting out on that last, great sled patrol'. *St Roch* survives in the Vancouver Maritime Museum, and in 1987 the Canadian Coast Guard commissioned an icebreaker in his honour. After a refit in 2000, the CCGS *Henry Larsen* is now capable of operating year-round in the High Arctic.

GALWAY BAY, 2009
JARLATH CUNNANE 1944-

Jarlath Cunnane leans past us to check the trim of the foresails. It's dawn off the west coast of Ireland. Our craft is a beautiful old Galway hooker and from below lift the smells of bacon and coffee. 'You're surely done by now lads', he says, 'cos I'm certain its time for breakfast'.

A grand, polar bear of a man, Cunnane looks as if he were born for a life at sea. He's a gentle soul and, I imagine, a wonderful guy to travel with. His eyes twinkle with songs and stories yet to be enjoyed. He built his first boat – a 14-foot dinghy – when he was still a teenager. Despite a busy professional life as the manager of major civil engineering projects across Ireland, he somehow found time to build himself a steel Van de Stadt 34, which he sailed to the Azores in 1990. Buoyed by this adventure, he chose to 'retire early and get a life'. 'Besides my ever-tolerant wife and our beautiful children', he tells me, 'this was the best decision I ever made!'

In 1997, he joined an Irish expedition recreating Shackleton's epic boat voyage across the Southern Ocean in the 22-foot lifeboat *James Caird*, building their replica boat himself. Most famously, Cunnane built and skippered *Northabout*, a 50-foot ice-strengthened aluminium yacht for his attempt to navigate the Northwest Passage. Despite encountering heavy ice, and unfathomable military bureaucracy, they completed the voyage in a record thirteen weeks. The crew returned to Ireland, leaving the boat in Alaska. But the challenge of the polar sea would tempt Cunnane once more. He decided to sail her home via the Northeast Passage, the 'Northern Sea Route' along the barren Russian coast. He finally completed this passage in 2005, having over-wintered in Siberia. In doing so *Northabout* became the first yacht to complete an east-to-west circumnavigation the Arctic Ocean. For his 'seamanship and adventure' Cunnane was rightly awarded the prestigious Blue Water Medal.

LONDON, 1848
SIR FRANCIS BEAUFORT 1774-1857

Born in County Meath, Francis Beaufort was the son of a wealthy local heiress and a Protestant clergyman with a passion for cartography. Having been rejected by a school in England on the grounds his Irish accent would corrupt the speech of the other boys, Beaufort determined to escape to sea. In 1789 he joined the Honourable East India Company ship *Vansittart* bound for Indonesia. While surveying the Gaspar Strait, near the South China Sea, the ship was wrecked, but Beaufort and most of the crew survived. He returned to England in time to be mobilised for war against France, rising from midshipman to commander. He served in the frigate *Aquilon* during the Battle of the Glorious First of June in 1794. He was later wounded in the Mediterranean while capturing the Spanish ship *San Josef*, receiving a blow to the head and 'several slugs in his body and arms'.

Nevertheless, he returned to active service and became captain in 1810. For leisure, he spent his days taking soundings, bearings and measuring shorelines. At night he perfected methods of astronomical observation to better determine longitude and latitude. In 1812 he explored the classical ruins of southern Anatolia, before being shot in the hip by a 'mob of fanatical Turks'. It was during these years, that Beaufort developed the first versions of his Wind Force Scale, which he was to use in his journals throughout his life, and for which he is best remembered today.

He returned to England and drew up the charts of his travels. In 1829, on the brink of retirement at the age of fifty-five, Beaufort became the Hydrographer of the Admiralty and held the post for the next twenty-five years. He transformed what was essentially a storage depôt into the finest surveying institution in the world. Many of their excellent charts are still used, over 150 years after they were created. He took over the administration of the great astronomical observatories at Greenwich and the Cape of Good Hope, he helped found the Royal Geographical Society, he established weather recording as a science and encouraged the development of the world's first tide tables. Perhaps even more spectacularly, Beaufort helped direct many of the great maritime endeavours of the age, including James Clark Ross's expedition to Antarctica and Robert Fitzroy's circumnavigation in the *Beagle*, with the young Charles Darwin in tow. Like many other patrons of exploration, Beaufort is remembered on charts all over the world: the Beaufort Sea in the Arctic, inlets in Western Australia and North Carolina, and a remote island in the Antarctic – a windswept lump of volcanic basalt, home to a colony of penguins.

Beaufort was made a rear admiral at the age of seventy-two but stayed on at the Hydrographic Office, working until 1855. Considering that he still carried a lead ball in his chest, had been knocked down by a runaway post office van, was deaf, and survived a heart attack at his desk, he was still in surprisingly good spirits. He was also keeping up his weather journal. Somewhat belatedly, he was knighted for his efforts in 1848. Shortly afterwards, in civilian dress, he posed for a photograph by John Mayall at his newly-opened London studio, the 'American Daguerreotype Institution'. This rare image is a coup in itself, for few others of Beaufort survive, but equally so as a perfect example of this pioneering photographic process. Beaufort died in 1857, just as this new technology was transforming the way people saw themselves. It would not be long before photography had travelled the globe.

LA JOLLA, 2010
WALTER MUNK 1917-

We join Walter Munk at his beautiful home in La Jolla, nestled in the cliffside, the Pacific a broad sweep of blue far below us. For a man who has devoted his life to the science of the sea it is a tranquil and appropriate place. His late wife's garden seems alive in the early morning sunshine and as we arrive, the phone rings. It's a call from Europe. The Royal Swedish Academy of Sciences has just made him their Crafoord Prize Laureate. He smiles. We sit and talk a little then make our way through a grove to a wooden bench overlooking the ocean. It was his wife's favourite spot, he says, her 'Martini Place'. 'It's nice to be here today. I haven't been able to come down here for a long time'.

A few paragraphs can't do justice to such a phenomenal life as Walter's. Born in Vienna, he graduated from Cal Tech in 1940, and enlisted in the fledgling ski troops. He worked for the US Navy and together with famed polar explorer Harald Sverdrup developed a method of ocean wave prediction. This knowledge was used in various Allied amphibious landings in Europe and the Pacific theatre. After the War, he joined the faculty of the Scripps Institution of Oceanography, where he is still teaching and researching ocean acoustics. He was Director for almost a quarter of a century. In explaining ocean circulation, tides and waves, and their role in our planet's dynamics, Professor Munk has extended humankind's scope for measuring and describing the oceans. He is, no doubt, a man touched with greatness, but with a warmth and humility that inspires all around him. It was a pleasure to meet him, if only for just a moment. 'I've been interested in all sorts of ocean things over the years,' he says, 'but I've still got so much to do. Perhaps I have been spreading myself too thin'.

SUNDERLAND, 1892

HARRY WATTS 1826-1913

Born in a Sunderland cellar to an invalid father and a mother who died when he was seven years old, Henry 'Harry' Watts was forced to grow up fast. The youngest of five children, by the age of nine he was one of the family breadwinners – running errands and collecting flotsam on the beach. By the time he was fourteen he was an apprentice sailor. He shipped first to Quebec and undertook a number of trading voyages bringing timber from Canada to Newcastle. He was three times ship-wrecked. A skilled and fearless swimmer, Watts soon found he had a particular aptitude for rescuing himself, and others, from stormy seas. In 1845 he rescued two men when a barge capsized in the Thames and two years later he helped six sailors escape from a boat that had been smashed by an anchor in Rotterdam. He returned to England and spent a number of years as a rigger, finding odd jobs in the docks and volunteering with the Sunderland lifeboat. In 1864 he used the diving-bell for the first time, laying ships' moorings in the River Wear and removing rocks from the harbour entrance. At considerable risk, and small reward, he was later employed in recovering cargo and raising wrecks from the sea floor.

After some thirty years of modest service, he was finally honoured with a medal from the Royal Humane Society and more awards would follow. In 1878, his medals were stolen from a church where they had been on display, but his supporters soon replaced them. The following year, he offered to assist in recovering the remains of casualties from the Tay Bridge collapse. He refused to be paid for his time, instead donating his wages to a charity for the bereaved. Quietly making his way home one night in 1892, without a

moment's hesitation, he swam to the rescue of a young boy who had fallen into the dock. The hero was so exhausted that he also had to be hauled out by a rope. Watts was sixty-six years old.

'He stands five feet nine inches in height, is straight as a pole, muscular and strong, and has a grip to the hand of him like a vice', ran one commentary. 'Reddish hair and beard, what one may call a fresh-weather complexion, keen blue eyes which look out bold and fearless from under the overhanging brows. He is now be-medalled about the breast, as if the grand old hero of a hundred fights'. 'Alter his dress', another admirer continued, 'and place a winged helmet on his head, and you have a true specimen of the old Vikings ... there is no mistaking the fact that he is a son of Neptune'. Though his looks may have faded in old age, his courtesy, politeness and humanity continued to earn him the love and respect of the people of the town in which he was born. During his life, Watts not only saved at least thirty-six people single-handedly, but he also participated in about 120 other rescue operations.

Heralded by a grateful public and with medals bestowed upon him, it is surprising that Watts is virtually unknown today. The Scottish-born industrialist Andrew Carnegie described meeting Watts in 1910, shortly before his death. 'I have today been introduced to a man who has, I think, the most ideal character of any man living on the face of the earth. I have shaken hands with a man who has saved many lives ... compared with his acts, military glory sinks into nothing. The hero who kills men is the hero of barbarism; the hero of civilization saves the lives of his fellows'.

TASMAN SEA, 2007
ANDREW McAULEY 1967-2007

In 2005, Andrew McAuley was named Australian Geographic Adventurer of the Year. A lifetime of travels had taken him to the remotest parts of the world, from his first ascent of Cerro La Pazz in Patagonia to the iceberg-choked seas of the Antarctic Peninsula. In 2003, he made the first direct kayak crossing of Bass Strait, paddling some 220km in thirty-five gruelling hours. The following year he pushed himself even further, making the first solo kayak crossing of the Gulf of Carpentaria. He was now set for the biggest challenge of all, to cross the Tasman Sea, alone, among some of the largest waves in the world.

His plan was to paddle from Fortescue Bay to New Zealand's Milford Sound, with the entire route below 40°S. It had never been dared before. In the middle of the Tasman, over 300 nautical miles from safety, McAuley took this self-portrait. An extract from his video diary, described the scene: 'Had a capsize yesterday. Big, big, big seas. Very scary, and it left me feeling very vulnerable. Makes you realise what a speck on the sea you are out here, you know. I'm right on the bloody edge...' Just thirty-five miles short of Milford Sound, the embrace of his wife and young son perhaps only a day away, his support team lost radio contact. He was within sight of land, but the seas were running high. He was never seen again.

Some time later, this haunting photograph was found on his camera's memory card, recovered in his partly flooded kayak. It would have meant a lot to Andrew, his wife Vicki tells me, to be in a book with so many people he admired. 'He died doing what he loved, the ocean was his inspiration, and I have to draw happiness from that. I find solace in the thought of the euphoria he would have experienced when he sighted the coast of New Zealand, with the first glimpse of mountains rising above the clouds'.

CONEY ISLAND, 1879
MATTHEW WEBB 1848-1883

Captain Matthew Webb was the first man to swim the English Channel. In 1875 most thought the feat impossible and it would be thirty-six years before anyone bothered to do it again. For his aquatic stunts, he would become famous on both sides of the Atlantic, turning swimming into a popular pastime. Born a doctor's son in Shropshire, Webb joined the merchant navy, serving in the East India and China trade. As a boy he had saved one of his brothers from drowning in the River Severn and while second mate on the Cunard steamship *Russia*, he attempted to rescue a man who had fallen overboard, diving into the waves in the mid-Atlantic. The man was never found, but Webb's daring won him a gold medal of the Royal Humane Society. Buoyed by public attention, he abandoned the sea-faring life to become the first professional swimmer.

The desire to swim across the Channel had started in 1862 when merchant seaman William Hoskins had drifted across on a bundle of straw. Others had attempted the crossing in all sorts of inflatable suits but tough tidal conditions, not to mention busy shipping, made the proposition a testing one. In 1873, Webb read a newspaper story about the failed swim of J.B. Johnson but felt sure that he could do better. He began training, first in Lambeth Baths, then in the cold waters of the Thames. Strong winds forced him to abandon a first attempt. For his second try in 1875 he was backed by three chase boats and smeared in porpoise oil. A jellyfish temporarily slackened his pace but he fortified himself in the water with a diet of beer, brandy and beef tea. He reached the beach in Calais after a swim of nearly 22 hours.

Webb's achievement hit the newspapers. London's newest celebrity, he gave performances of his aquatic prowess in the Westminster Royal Aquarium. He took part in swimming galas on Brighton Beach, dressed in a skullcap and greased tights. On one occasion, he raced George Wade – a railroad engineer from Brooklyn, so called the 'champion ocean swimmer in America' – and won a prize of a thousand dollars. Having licensed the merchandising rights to his name, his face appeared on souvenir plates, china pots, matchboxes and piano music. His book *The Art of Swimming* became a bestseller and he travelled to America to seek his fortune. To the delight of the punters who bet on him, he managed to swim from Sandy Hook to Manhattan Beach in just over 8 hours. And it would have been quicker, but for the time he spent shooting rockets and performing for spectators in the surf.

This rare photograph was taken shortly after this swim, to advertise his future stunts. A journalist from *The New York Times*, caught up with him just before he jumped into the rolling Atlantic. 'Webb looked ready to undertake any trial of endurance. He seems more a man of great natural strength than one who has built himself up with gymnastics. His skin is rough and bears a great many pimples and blotches owing to salt water. His face is well bronzed and roughened, and his light-coloured mustache looks bleached'.

Though many press stories were written about him, public interest waned. In an effort to bolster attendance for shows, Webb decided for immortality by swimming across the Whirlpool Rapids at Niagara Falls. Local hotels sponsored the event and a special train from New York was laid on for sightseers. Gamblers rushed to place their bets. Odds of three to two were offered that he would not enter the water at all. Sadly, Webb did not make it out alive. His body was found a few days later, four miles downstream, its features disfigured by a large gash to the head and his flesh bloated to double the usual size. He was identified by a tiny, almost indiscernible, blue anchor tattooed on his arm. In 1909, a huge memorial was unveiled in his hometown of Dawley. On it reads the short inscription: 'Nothing great is easy'. He left a widow and two young children.

SEAL BEACH, 2010
LYNNE COX 1957-

It is likely the ocean has never had such an enthusiastic and engaging champion as it has in author and open-water swimmer Lynne Cox. She meets us at dawn on California's Seal Beach. There's a storm coming, the swell is rising, and in the early morning sunshine the surfers are running out to greet the waves. It's a familiar scene for Cox – she trains here almost every day of the year, at least when she's not swimming in some far-flung corner of the globe.

Almost forty years ago now, she broke the world record for swimming the English Channel. She was the first to swim across the Strait of Magellan from Tierra Del Fuego to the Chilean mainland, the Strait of Gibraltar from Morocco to Spain and to swim around the Cape of Good Hope, among countless other inspirational adventures. She is perhaps most famous for being the first to swim the frigid Bering Strait from America to the Soviet Union in 1987 – an accomplishment which eased Cold War tensions, bringing praise from both Ronald Reagan and Mikhail Gorbachev. Most recently, she became the first to swim a mile in Antarctica – and to make it out alive – causing the US press to describe her as a 'force of nature'. She smiles when I remind her of it.

Cox doesn't take to the water for fame or notoriety. She does it, most simply, to encourage people to engage with the ocean world. 'I use my swims as a way to reach out to people in different lands', she explains, as we share breakfast after the shoot. 'Swimming, genuinely, can bridge distance and help to further international relationships. The ocean is the home of life. It's beautiful beyond words, fragile and powerful. The ocean should be the passage to peace and a common understanding. We all share in the sea, and we all must be part of the solution to the problems we've created'.

ARCTIC OCEAN, 1934

OTTO SCHMIDT 1891-1956

Mathematician, diplomat, geophysicist and explorer, Otto Yulyevich Schmidt is a towering figure within the history of the Soviet North. Robust and formidable – at well over six feet five inches tall and sporting the huge, bushy beard he had cultivated since university days – he came to personify the public image of the perfect polar explorer. Dubbed 'Commissar of Ice' and 'Grandfather Frost' by the Soviet press, Schmidt had only to enter a room, one admirer recalled, 'for everyone immediately to feel this man knew everything, understood everything, and could do anything'.

Born in Mogilev, a city now in modern Belarus, Schmidt was descended from German peasants but was quick to make the most of his chances in life. He joined the Bolsheviks in 1918 and distinguished himself as an administrator during the Civil War. His efforts caught the eye of Lenin himself, who called Schmidt 'our Professor Otto' and described him as 'irrepressible'. He mastered more than a dozen foreign languages and steeped himself in literature. In the mid 1940s, Schmidt put forward a new hypothesis for the formation of the Earth and the Solar System, which he continued to develop until his unexpected death in 1956.

But it was work in the Arctic that would make Schmidt world famous. In 1929 and 1930 he led expeditions on the steam icebreaker *Georgy Sedov*, exploring the Kara Sea and establishing the first scientific research station on Franz Josef Land. In 1932, his voyage on the sealing steamer *Sibiryakov* with Captain Vladimir Voronin, non-stop from Arkhangelsk to the Pacific, made the first transit of the Northeast Passage without overwintering. That December he was appointed head of *Glavsevmorput*, the 'Main Administration of the Northern Sea Route', effectively a 'state within a state'

charged with overseeing some two million square miles of Russian territory. The following year, he undertook a second passage in *Chelyuskin*. After leaving Murmansk in August 1933, the steamship managed to navigate the bulk of the route before it was caught in the ice, drifted, and later sunk off Siberia. Escaping the wreck of their ship, the crew built a makeshift airstrip on the shifting sea ice and had to rebuild it thirteen times before they were dramatically airlifted to safety. His crew embarked on a long trip to Moscow on the Trans-Siberian Railway, making appearances in dozens of cities along the way. Schmidt, meanwhile, flew to Alaska and began his own triumphal tour. He was fêted in New York, spoke to the nation on special radio shows, he even lunched with President Roosevelt. In Europe he appeared in Paris, Prague and Warsaw, returning to Moscow just as his fellow 'Chelyuskinites' rolled into town. In the riotous celebrations in Red Square, Schmidt was embraced by Stalin himself.

The Northern Sea Route was officially opened and commercial exploitation began in 1935. The following year, part of the Soviet Baltic Fleet made its first passage to the Pacific where an armed conflict with Japan was looming. In 1937, Schmidt supervised a pioneering airborne expedition that established the first ice-station at the North Pole. Its four scientists were rescued the following year, drifting off the coast of Greenland, and were given another huge welcome in Moscow. Schmidt was made a 'Hero of the Soviet Union' for his feats in service of the state. His own words captured the spirit of the times: 'We do not chase after records, although we break not a few upon the way. We do not look for adventures, although we experience them with every step. Our goal is to study the North for the good of the entire USSR'.

LONDON, 2009
ANDREW LAMBERT 1956-

Framed for this portrait by the magnificent Navy Staircase at Somerset House in London, Professor Andrew Lambert describes for us the past glories of the Admiralty and the vagaries of sea power. As engaging in person as he is impressive on the page, Lambert is rightly considered one of the finest maritime historians of his generation. When asked whose ocean achievements he most admires, his reply is perfect: 'Well, all those who go down to the sea in ships, to make a passage, to defend their nation, to save lives or, quite simply, to see what is out there. The sea means so much to so many people'.

Lambert is currently Laughton Professor of Naval History in the Department of War Studies at King's College. He studied first in London, before teaching at the Royal Naval Staff College in Greenwich and the Royal Military Academy, Sandhurst. He was, for over ten years, Hon Secretary of the Navy Records Society. He has written best-selling books on a range of ocean subjects, from grand strategy in the Crimean War to scientific surveys in the Arctic. His biography of Nelson, completed in 2004, just before the bicentenary of the Battle of Trafalgar, won him wide praise and the following year he was invited to give a special lecture in the small church at Burnham Thorpe, the Norfolk village where his hero Nelson was born. Despite the glittering achievements of his academic career, it was, Lambert tells me, his proudest moment.

RDPIII   FUJI RDP

RDPIII ⬭ 26·

Pradelle & Young

283. REGENT ST.
LONDON. W.

LONDON, 1888
SIR EDWARD INGLEFIELD 1820-1894

Cheltenham-born and Portsmouth educated, Edward Augustus Inglefield, was the eldest son of a distinguished rear admiral. He went to sea at fourteen, taking part in action off the Syrian coast in 1840. He was for a short time in the West Indies and on the Royal Yacht. In 1852, Inglefield commanded the private steamer *Isabel* in a summer expedition to the Arctic in search of Sir John Franklin. He went northward again in 1853, returning that autumn with the news that Captain Robert McClure had discovered a northwest passage. In 1854, with HMS *Phoenix*, he made a third search voyage, bringing back some remarkable photographs, among the first to be taken in the Arctic.

In 1855, he was appointed to *Firebrand* in the Black Sea and took part in the siege of Sevastopol. In the early 1860s he commanded *Majestic*, the coastguard ship at Liverpool and later cruised the Mediterranean in the ironclad *Prince Consort*. He was also for some time superintendent of Malta Dockyard and British naval attaché in Washington. In 1885 he was put on the retired list, but was not lost for things to keep him busy. A charismatic man of cultivated taste, he was a prolific author, an inventor of anchors and hydraulic steering gear (with a workshop in his beloved garden), and an exceptional amateur artist – some of his paintings, including portraits of the Queen, were exhibited at the Royal Academy. He was finally nominated a KCB in June 1887, during celebrations for the Golden Jubilee, and this photograph was taken shortly afterward.

The handsome embroidery on Inglefield's cuffs show the insignia of a full Admiral, his epaulettes, just discernable, bear Victoria's cipher crown, a sword and baton crossed, and a cluster of eight-pointed stars. On his chest are various campaign medals and the distinctive jewelled star as Knight Commander of the Order of the Bath, its small gold Maltese cross suspended from his collar with a crimson ribbon. After Inglefield's death in 1894, this photograph was used as the basis of a notable portrait by John Collier, an artist celebrated for painting the heroes of the day, including the future King George V as master of Trinity House, Lord Kitchener of Khartoum and Charles Darwin. Lady Franklin described Inglefield as 'an open-hearted, sincere person, pretending to no exalted sentiments of self-devotion, but upright, honourable, straightforward and kind-hearted'.

GOTHENBURG, 2009
SKIP NOVAK 1952-

High-latitude master-mariner and entrepreneur, James Vladimir Novak strikes a pose in a Gothenburg studio. His portrait was captured by Jan Söderström for technical sail clothing manufacturer Sailracing. For a sailor who never takes the easy way, who seems to live continually on the edge, it's rare to find 'Skip' in these comfortable surroundings. The following day, he grabs his kit and heads back to Antarctica.

Now one of Sailracing's testing team, Novak is best known for his participation in four Whitbread Round the World Races. In his first year, at the age of just twenty-five, he navigated the British cutter *King's Legend* to second place. As skipper of *Independent Endeavour* in 1979, he won the commemorative Parmelia Race from Plymouth to Freemantle Australia, and he led Simon Le Bon's *Drum* in the 1985-86 Whitbread. In 1989 he found himself project manager and skipper of *Fazisi*, the first Soviet entry. Wishing to combine sailing with his passion for mountaineering, he built the expedition vessel *Pelagic* in 1987 and has since spent over two decades sailing in high latitudes, developing his adventure charter and logistic support company Pelagic Expeditions.

In 1997, he navigated the French catamaran *Explorer* to a sailing record in the Transpac race from Los Angeles to Honolulu and the following year, as co-skipper with the visionary yachtsman Bruno Peyron, he broke the sailing record from Yokohama to San Francisco. Countless other race wins followed. In 2002, Novak led the construction of a 23-metre purpose-built expedition vessel, *Pelagic Australis*, to augment his charter operations. She is considered the 'Rolls Royce of the high latitude charter fleet'. When asked about his success, his advice to young sailors is simple: 'Don't think about a career in the beginning, have the courage to let that evolve naturally. Be prepared to work for free and grab every opportunity offered. Take the voyages that carry a degree of risk and uncertainty, otherwise, to quote Sterling Hayden, "you are doomed to a routine traverse"'.

SYDNEY, 1950
FRANK HURLEY 1885-1962

The pioneering 'camera artist' and war photographer, Frank Hurley works on a model ship, snug in retirement at his home on the Collaroy Plateau, a quiet suburb just north of Sydney. It was, perhaps, a far cry from the intrepid adventures that had taken him with his cameras all over the globe. Yet, the rooms of his cottage were crowded with memories and mementoes – tribal artifacts from the jungles of New Guinea and Java, relics from the deserts of the Middle East – and underneath all this was his basement retreat, the dark-room, with its strangely-shaped white sinks and shelves crowded with glass plates and chemicals. Hurley's modest sitting room was dressed with prints of his most famous photographs, and in this candid family portrait one can glimpse some of those taken on his voyages to Antarctica. Each was a window to another world; into the vast ice floes of the Southern Ocean and a golden age of polar exploration.

James Francis Hurley was born at Glebe, Sydney, the second son of a printer and a mother of French descent. At thirteen 'Frank' ran away from school, first working in a steel mill and then the docks. At night he studied at the local technical college and, becoming interested in photography, he saved enough money to buy his own Kodak box camera. In 1905 he joined a postcard business and the quality of his work, not to mention his extravagant risk-taking, soon brought him to wider attention. In 1911, Douglas Mawson invited him to be official photographer on the Australian Antarctic Expedition and for two years he worked under extreme conditions, taking both still photographs and movie film. Back in Sydney, he assembled his footage and presented it to the public as *Home of the Blizzard*, the first complete polar feature film. His fame grew and he joined Sir Ernest Shackleton on the *Endurance* expedition, a voyage that turned into an epic of survival. His photographs of the saga are among the finest ever taken in the South.

As the world turned to war, Hurley offered his talents to the Australian Imperial Force as its official photographer, with the honorary rank of captain. Away from the horrors of the Western Front, in Cairo he met a young opera-singer, the daughter of an Indian Army officer. They were married in 1918 after a ten-day whirlwind romance. In peacetime, Hurley's innovative talents took him to exotic locations all over the world – making long expeditions to the Torres Strait and to Papua, and rejoining Mawson for another research voyage. His films from this expedition, *Southward Ho!* and *Siege of the South*, are classics in adventure film-making.

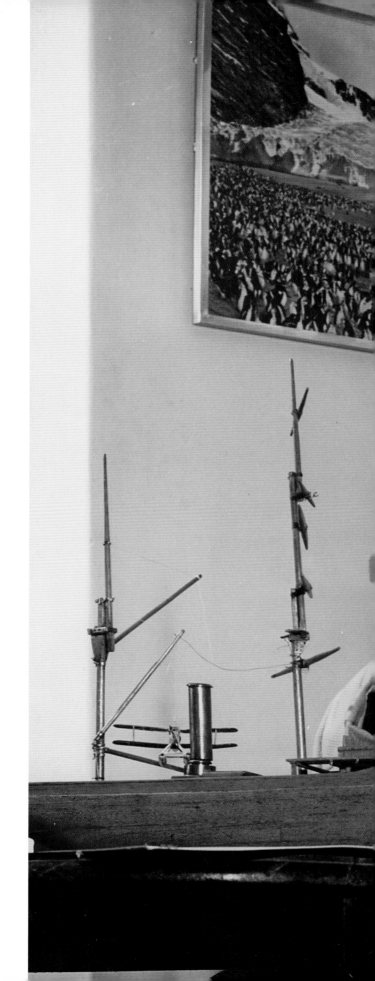

GURNARD, 2009
RICK TOMLINSON 1958-

Marine photographer Rick Tomlinson is best known for capturing the Southern Ocean at its most treacherous from the decks of various yachts in the Whitbread Round the World Race. He has trained his cameras at all manner of activity at sea: from America's Cup campaigns and assignments for the RNLI, through to private polar expeditions and regattas the world over. A modest man, through his talent and his affinity for the ocean he now stands as one of the best in the business.

Born in 1958, Rick grew up on the Isle of Man, where he spent much of his time on the water racing dinghies. His enthusiasm for photography began while he was boatbuilding and sailing, particularly with his friend Nick Keig. Some years later, they would both be awarded with the RNLI Bronze Medal for saving the lives of two fishermen off the coast of Northern Ireland. He eventually headed south to join the build team of the Maxi Colt Cars. The yacht ended up in the hands of Duran Duran rock star Simon Le Bon with the new name *Drum*. After a near fatal roll in the Fastnet Race when *Drum*'s keel broke off, the boat was quickly repaired for the start of the Whitbread in 1985. The management suggested someone should take photos – and as one of the crew, Rick jumped at the chance. Though he set off with just one Nikon camera and 20 rolls of film, his photos were a huge success. His trademark long exposure night shots of the Southern Ocean redefined onboard photography.

He would eventually sail in four Whitbread races, including a commission for *National Geographic* in 1997. More recently, he was Official Photographer to the GBR Challenge at the America's Cup in Auckland and the Volvo Ocean Race in 2008-09. We catch up with Rick on the slipway in front of his home at Gurnard, tucked away on the north coast of the Isle of Wight. It's a gloomy Autumn evening with not much activity on the Solent, but come the summer this stretch of water is alive with sail. With a perfect view from his living room, and a chase boat ready offshore, Rick is never far from this action. That is, if he's not leaning out a helicopter shooting yachts on the other side of the world.

LONDON, 1853
THOMAS POTTER COOKE 1786-1864

Thomas Potter Cooke was one of the most famous actors of the early Victorian stage. His huge popularity is comparable to the film stars of today. In a theatre career that spanned almost sixty years he received acclaim for his performances of villains, monsters, smugglers and pirates, yet it was for his numerous roles as a heroic sailor that he was most admired. For the genteel classes at least, sailors had been fearful figures: unruly, unpredictable, engaging in day-long drunken carousing and brawling in the streets. Cooke's characters offered a more acceptable image of what a sailor *ought* to be. The new Jack Tar was respectful, still a little boisterous, but willing and fearless when duty called.

Cooke was born in Marylebone on 23 April 1786 – Shakespeare's birthday – the son of a well-known London doctor. As a child he was sent to the Marine Society's school but soon went to sea. He served in *Raven* when he was just ten years old, giving his age as thirteen on the muster roll. He was at the Siege of Toulon and saw action at the Battle of Cape St Vincent in 1797. Coming home he was wrecked off Cuxhaven and survived by clinging to the wreckage of his ship for almost two days. He contracted rheumatic fever, from which he nearly died, and resigned from the Navy. Two years later he rejoined the service and took part in various engagements against the French until the Peace of Amiens in 1802 brought hostilities, briefly, to an end.

Cooke was a sailor born for the stage. He joined a travelling circus, arranged pantomimes, before landing a job as stage manager for the Surrey Theatre. He leapt into public prominence in 1820, playing the demonic lead in *The Vampire* at the English Opera House and fast became a master of the villainous and supernatural, winning more plaudits as the cursed navigator Vanderdecken in *The Flying Dutchman* and the mute monster in

the sensational *Fate of Frankenstein*. His most famous role of all, however, was as the loyal sailor William in *Black-Eyed Susan*, which opened in 1829. It was so popular that Cooke often performed twice a night; first at the Surrey Theatre, before jumping – sometimes still in costume – into a waiting cab to be taken back across the river to appear at Covent Garden.

In 1853, sixty-eight years old, Cooke was persuaded to come out of retirement and reprise his nautical roles. Later that year he was photographed at the Mayall studio – likely where this stunning, rare image was also created – and his portrait was circulated as an engraving in *The Illustrated London News*. Still playful and energetic, and looking like a man half his age, audiences were overjoyed. 'He was the best sailor that ever trod the boards', ran one typical review, 'and his every look, gesture, and motion are redolent of the blue water and the lower deck'. His popular performances – with his manly figure, brandishing a cutlass, defying the enemy and rescuing females in distress from beneath the folds of the Union Jack – had established the popular image of the sailor.

One of Cooke's final performances was at Covent Garden in 1860 for the benefit of the Dramatic College, a retirement home for actors. His fame had brought rich reward but his thoughts had always been for others. His wife's death in 1863 affected him deeply and he never really recovered. On his death the following year, he left £2,000 to provide a prize for 'the best Drama on a Nautical or National subject', with an extra fund set aside for a riotous annual dinner. At his funeral, his coffin was borne by a procession of carriages and more than a thousand people, with old sailors, actors and admirers alike gathering to pay their respects. 'Mr T.P. Cooke', one tribute declared, was 'the most popular British Tar that this country produced since the immortal Nelson!'

ATLANTIC OCEAN, 1992
BRUNO PEYRON 1955-

Off New York in the summer of 1992, maverick French sailing hero Bruno Peyron relaxes for a portrait during preparations for his solo Atlantic voyage. Later that year, he astonished everyone by crossing the ocean in just nine days. A pioneer of multihull racing, Peyron did not rest for a moment after this triumph but turned his talents to circumnavigation.

The Jules Verne Trophy was devised to beat the record of 109 days set during the first edition of the Vendée Globe race in 1990. The rules are simple: a boat of any size, naturally propelled, to start and finish on an imaginary line between the Brittany island of Ushant and the Lizard in Cornwall, must sail nonstop round the world, leaving the Cape of Good Hope and Cape Horn to port, and do this all in under eighty days. In 1993, having mastered the Southern Ocean in his epic catamaran *Commodore Explorer*, Peyron became the inaugural winner by sprinting up the Atlantic to make it home in just 79 days. In March 2005, sailing with his crew in *Orange II*, Peyron broke the outright round-the-world sailing record again. He completed the 27,000 nautical mile circumnavigation in a breathtaking 50 days, 16 hours and 20 minutes. 'It's more a moving experience than a joyful one', Peyron said after crossing the line.

Bruno was born into an adventurous family with salt in their veins. His uncle was a yacht racer, his father the master of an ocean-going supertanker, and the family learned to sail in the bay of La Baule. His brother Loïck has become a well-respected multihull ocean racer in his own right, with forty-three Atlantic crossings to his name; their young brother Stéphane became the first to windsurf his way across the Atlantic in 1987, and he now travels the world as a film-maker.

In 2006, Bruno reclaimed the outright 24-hour distance record, on his opening day of a new trans-Atlantic challenge. Setting out from Ambrose Light, New York, he covered some 766.8 nautical miles, with a staggering average speed of 31.95 knots. In doing so he would also win the trans-Atlantic crewed record, reaching Lizard Point in 4 days, 8 hours, 23 minutes and 54 seconds, a time once thought impossible. Amazingly, it has now been bettered twice, by the French sailors Franck Cammas and Pascal Bidégorry. Though there must be more to life than simply increasing its speed, Peyron's achievements are testament to his skill and tenacity as one of the world's best ocean racers.

PARIS, 1953
ALAIN BOMBARD 1924-2005

Dr Alain Bombard was a mercurial French physician and biologist who became famous in Europe for drifting across the Atlantic in a small inflatable raft. Born in Paris, it was said he became interested in ocean survival techniques in 1951 when he was rescued during an unsuccessful attempt to cross the English Channel. He and a friend made do with a half-kilogram of butter for five days. He was then inspired to develop ways for people lost in small boats to survive on even less.

Although it was a common belief that drinking saltwater would kill, Bombard came to the conclusion that drinking about a pint of seawater a day, along with raw fish and a dollop of plankton, could provide the nutrition necessary to keep a shipwrecked sailor alive for weeks. Not one to hide behind his research, after six months of experimenting with fishy juices – 'the wonderful foodstuff offered by the sea' – Bombard acquired a 15-foot rubber dinghy, which he named *L'Heretique*, and stocked it with fishing tackle, bags to catch rain water, a sextant, and a compass. He set out alone from Casablanca in 1952. Sixty-five days, and some 4,000 storm-tossed miles later, 'constantly dreaming of beer', he was washed ashore on a sandy beach in Barbados. He had endured terror, shark attack, hallucinations, and had grown desperate in his solitude. This stylish portrait is by Martha Holmes, commissioned for a *Life* magazine feature shortly after his return, by plane, to France. 'Bombard was a rotund, cheerful doctor with a fantastic theory – that man could live for a long period on the sea alone. He set out to test this theory and wound up as a gaunt figure with the look of the Ancient Mariner'. He summed up his ocean adventure as 'a starving, thirsty hell'.

Almost instantly, his folly was called into question. Half way out in the middle of the ocean, it was discovered, Bombard had stopped to take a meal on a British cargo ship. Others claimed he had stowed fresh water in his little boat. Testing his results a few years later, Hannes Lindemann, a German doctor and long-distance kayaker found he couldn't survive on Bombard's diet and he was quick to tell the newspapers so. Regardless of the validity of his methods, Bombard's adventure had been a courageous one. He spent the rest of his life in politics, becoming a thorn in the side of the establishment. When a Frenchman, Guy Delage, claimed to have swam across the Atlantic in 1995, journalists turned to Bombard for comment. 'I will certainly refrain from tearing him apart', he said in an interview with *The New York Times*, 'since people have always made fun of me'.

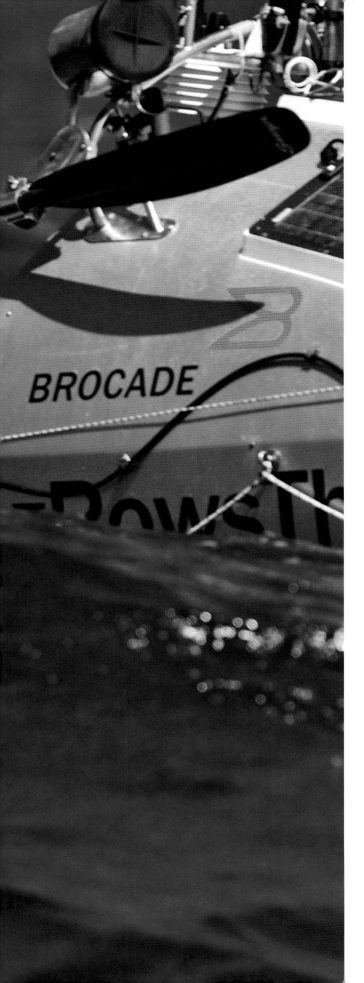

BROCADE

PACIFIC
OCEAN, 2008
ROZ SAVAGE 1967 -

British rower and environmental campaigner Rosalind Savage pulls on her oars, in high seas and sunshine, as she approaches the Hawaiian island of Oahu. It was the final day of the first stage in her solo trans-Pacific row. By her own admission a latecomer to adventure, Roz worked as a management consultant for eleven years before realising there was more to life than 'a steady income and a house in the suburbs'. Frustrated, she set out in a new direction – in a rowboat. In 2005, she competed in the 3,000-mile Atlantic Rowing Race. In 2008, she became the first woman to row solo from California to Hawaii. She continued her Pacific bid the following year, by rowing from Hawaii to Kiribati, the tiny island nation lying on the Equator, 'about as far from anywhere as it's possible to be', she says. The third and final stage of her Pacific row takes place in Spring 2010, when she attempts to row solo from Kiribati to Australia.

Roz is a now a UN 'Climate Hero' and an ambassador for the BLUE Oceans and Climate Project. Her time at sea leaves her in no doubt about the emergency that our planet faces: 'We have trashed the oceans. Utterly. Even a thousand miles from land, it is a plastic soup'. She first went out on the ocean in search of solitude and self-fulfilment, but now she feels it must be the source of bringing people together, not setting them apart. 'The oceans connect us all, they remind us that no nation is independent. We all share this fragile ecosystem, and it's our duty to find a common solution'.

SANDY HOOK, 1920
SIR THOMAS LIPTON 1848-1931

Sir Thomas Johnstone Lipton, First Baronet, Knight Commander of the Royal Victorian Order – a printer's errand boy made merchant millionaire – is long remembered as the biggest loser in the history of yacht racing. Though he challenged the America's Cup a total of five times and was defeated five times, he was widely admired. Without his dynamism and finance, not to forget his sheer persistence, the Cup would not have endured to become the pre-eminent sporting contest it is today.

Born to a poor Irish family in Glasgow, at fifteen Lipton emigrated to the United States on a steam packet, and soon discovered the world of business. He returned to Scotland with considerable savings and opened a grocer's shop, which, thanks to his flair for commerce, quickly prospered. He was soon specializing in the overseas trade and in 1890 acquired land in Ceylon where he began cultivating his world-famous 'Lipton tea'. He was knighted by Queen Victoria in 1898 and it was her son, the future King Edward VII, who introduced Lipton to the fashionable world of yachting.

Between 1899 and 1930 he challenged the holders of the America's Cup, through the Royal Ulster Yacht Club, five times with his elegant yachts, each named *Shamrock*. In 1903, at his third attempt, Lipton was bested by Herreshoff's cutter *Reliance*. 'They tell me I have a beautiful boat. I don't want a beautiful boat. What I want is a boat to lift the Cup!' Returning in 1920 with *Shamrock IV*, Lipton went closest to making Cup history, winning the first two races against *Resolute*. It was the first race taken by a challenger since *Livonia* won in 1871. Lipton watched on in excitement from *Erin*, his motor yacht, where this candid photograph was taken. Having won two of the best-of-five races, *Shamrock* only needed one more, but she then promptly lost the next three in a row, and with it the Cup. Lipton returned again in 1930, but his dreams were dashed by the Burgess-designed *Enterprise*, one of the finest yachts ever built.

Though failure must have been agonising for Lipton, there was some sweetness to defeat. His well-publicised efforts to win the Cup made his tea brand famous throughout America. When he died in London in 1931, he bequeathed the majority of his massive fortune to his native city of Glasgow, including his yachting trophies, which are now on display at the Kelvingrove Art Gallery. But, for Lipton, the America's Cup would remain elusive.

LONDON, 2009
JOHN BERTRAND 1946-

Master yachtsman John Bertrand sits at the kitchen table in his sister's London home. His thoughts are elsewhere; a steak sizzles on the barbeque in the garden. Bertrand was only eight when he and his brother got their first sailing dinghy. He had already spent a summer experimenting with an old hulk, with a parachute their mother had fashioned into a sail. It was the beginning of a life at sea that would see him become the greatest skipper in Australia, perhaps one of the finest in the world. But now it's time for lunch.

Following success at the Olympics, Bertrand went on to crew in America's Cup challenges, first on *Southern Cross* in 1974 and then *Australia* in 1980. He had served his time, it was only natural he would be made skipper for 1983. From that moment, the thirty-seven year old was dedicated to winning. Between *Australia II*'s launching and the final day of reckoning off Newport, he was to race her against boats of all sizes almost three hundred times. His words to his crew were simple: 'Spit blood if you have to, but we are going to attain a standard that will put us not only in front of the Americans but twenty years ahead!'

With nearly 500 million people watching across the world, *Australia II* came from behind to prevail four races to three, ending 132 years of American supremacy. The New York Yacht Club had dominated the event since 1851, but Bertrand changed all that, revitalising the sport in the process. In 1987, the defeated American skipper Dennis Conner, sailing under his home San Diego colours, became the first man to win back the prize. In future years, teams from New Zealand and Switzerland, drawing the best sailors from all over the planet, would compete for, and win, the Cup. On the water, at least, the competition still remains the very best in world sailing.

LONG ISLAND SOUND, 1967
EMIL MOSBACHER 1922-1997

Emil 'Bus' Mosbacher Jnr poses at the helm of the new 12-metre sloop *Intrepid*. Designed by the legendary Olin Stephens, *Intrepid* was built by the Minneford Yacht Yard and launched in 1967. Mosbacher was photographed by Rosenfeld and Sons later that summer, putting the new yacht through her paces. *Intrepid*'s design was radical and innovative – her rudder was separated from the stumpy keel and most of the winches were moved below decks enabling a low boom to make the mainsail more efficient. She remains one of the most famous racing yachts of all time. Redesigned by Britton Chance, for a second America's Cup outing, she defeated the Australian challenger *Gretel II* in 1970. Though she was the last classic wooden boat to defend the Cup, she remained competitive even against the new breed of aluminium 12-metre yachts. Redesigned again, this time by Stephens, she was back for a third time in 1974, though lost in the final race of the defender trials to the *Courageous*, which would go on to win the Cup that year with naval architect Ted Hood at the helm.

The son of a Wall Street stockbroker, Mosbacher led a charmed life overseeing his family's vast oil and real estate business. As a child, he sailed on Long Island Sound and progressed from one class of vessel to the next, winning countless prizes along the way. He found his forte in 33-foot sloop racing. Such was his dominance he won eight consecutive season championships in the International Class during the 1950s. He won attention for his handling of the aging yacht *Vim*, in the America's Cup selection trials of 1958, and in 1962 he was invited to take command of the sloop *Weatherly* and make her match-fit. Ever the keen-eyed perfectionist, Mosbacher did some calculations and removed what he considered to be excess weight, 'from a two-pound wind gauge that had perched atop the 90-foot mast to the previous skipper's pipe rack'. He saved more than half a ton and was then able to put lead in her keel for greater stability in strong winds. *Weatherly* was selected to defend the Cup, which she won despite a tough Australian challenge.

Though Mosbacher declared 'never again', by 1968 he was back at the helm of *Intrepid*. After fending off another team of Australian contenders he won the Cup a second time. In later life, Mosbacher forged a profitable career as a diplomat, company director, civil servant and racehorse owner. It was sailing, however, that remained his defining pleasure. 'Most of yacht racing is study, work and development', he once said. 'There are no radical breakthroughs, like suddenly discovering you can hit a golf ball farther if you use the back of your club. It is tactics, strategy, organization and a happy association with nice people'. Though he is rightly regarded as one of the toughest of the Cup skippers, his aggressive tactics were matched by a subtle understanding of the ocean.

HUNTINGTON BEACH, 2003
KELLY SLATER 1972-

Passionate fans of all sports love to debate 'who's best?' Surfers don't usually spend much time on subjects like this, but ask anyone and the answer is always the same. If you gauge it by competitions won and surfing innovations, or simply by speed, power and flair, one man stands head and shoulders above the rest – Kelly Slater. 'One part competitive animal and the other natural-born talent, Slater is hard to beat and, to date, impossible to beat consistently'. He has been crowned World Champion a record nine times, including five consecutive titles from 1994 through 1998. This simple portrait was captured on California's Huntington Beach, as Slater was supporting the US Open of Surfing. It was a contest he first won as part of a team back in 1992. Ten years later, after an epic career on the waves, he would be inducted at Huntington into the 'Surfing Walk of Fame'.

Slater had earned himself some time off – avoiding competitions, he hung out on great reef breaks in tropical locations the world over, he played his guitar and formed a band, he dated a string of beautiful women and found himself the focus of the tabloid press. But then, like heroes of other sports, the veteran came roaring back from retirement. The sea was calling him. In 2008, he won his ninth world title at the Billabong Pro in Mundaka, Spain, proving to everyone that he still had what it takes, and much more besides. It was a sublime victory, in some ways transcending the sport itself. And, like the waves, the eulogies rolled in. 'To watch Slater surf is to be mesmerized by a blend of suppleness, power and elegance', ran one commentary, 'his surfing is so fluid and gymnastic that it's as if he inhabits the ocean, rather than merely visits it'. Everyone is in agreement, 'Slater's competitive supremacy and mastery of the art of riding the ocean earns him the moniker *living legend*'. It is difficult to call the most dominant surfer of all time anything else.

OSLO, 1937
FELIX VON LUCKNER 1881-1966

Felix Graf von Luckner poses for a portrait shortly before leaving on his yacht for a voyage round the world. He would return just before the outbreak of war, having crossed the South Pacific and the Indian Ocean, returning to Europe by way of the Suez Canal. Known popularly as the 'Sea Devil', Luckner captained the merchant raider *Seeadler* during the First World War. He was a dashing character, who fought his enemy both with flair and fairness.

Born near Dresden in 1881, Luckner ran away to sea as a cabin boy on a Russian ship bound for Australia. In Fremantle he jumped ship and for the next few years tried his hand at all sorts of jobs: as lighthouse keeper, magician, kangaroo hunter, circus worker, fisherman, barman and professional boxer. Eventually, he returned to Germany and enrolled in a navigation training school, before joining the steamer *Petropolis*. In 1904, he volunteered for the Imperial German Navy and later served on the gunboat SMS *Panther* off the West African coast. He commanded a gun turret at the Battle of Jutland, aboard the battleship *Kronprinz*.

But it was his command of the three-masted windjammer *Seeadler*, 'Sea Eagle', that brought him international renown. He sank fourteen ships, with the loss of only one life, among both his crews and the enemy. Luckner was later captured after his ship was wrecked on a coral reef and held as a prisoner of war on Motuihe Island, off New Zealand. In the 1920s he rigged a Norwegian schooner, to become the first training ship of the German Navy. American broadcaster Lowell Thomas, famed for his accounts of Lawrence of Arabia, wrote a book about him that brought his adventures to a wide audience. Luckner later bought the schooner *Vaterland* and set out on a goodwill circumnavigation. In America he was received with a hero's welcome and gave hundreds of lectures. He was awarded the freedom of the City of San Francisco, while Henry Ford presented him with a new motorcar.

An extremely strong man – famed for his ability to tear up telephone directories or bend coins between his fingers – he was also admired for his tenderness, compassion and moral courage. During the Second World War, Hitler tried to use him for propaganda, though Luckner resisted and found his bank account frozen. In 1945, he negotiated with American forces and prevented the destruction of Halle by air attack. After the end of the war, Luckner moved to Sweden, where he lived in Malmö until his death. His body was returned for burial in Hamburg, with the overwhelming sympathy of the public and the press worldwide. One American paper reported: 'The gentleman pirate, Felix Count von Luckner was the German *good guy*!'

WELLS-NEXT-THE-SEA, 2009
FRANK DYE 1928-

'Why would anyone want to take to the open sea in a sailing dinghy for enjoyment? For the past 30 years, Frank and Margaret Dye have not only been explaining why, but also asking *Why Not?*' Thus ran an article, back in 1989, when Frank was elected into small boat sailing's Hall of Fame after a lifetime of maritime adventure. He smiles at the recollection. Some men thought him mad to make such perilous trips in his 15-foot Wayfarer dinghy, crossing bodies of water that intimidate even the largest vessels and the most experienced mariners. He has sailed in the wake of his ocean heroes, the Vikings, on voyages from Scotland across the North Atlantic to Iceland. On his second major passage, a North Sea crossing from Scotland to Norway, Frank and his companion, Bill Brockbank, survived four capsizes and a broken mast during a force-9 gale. They did not do it for fame, or notoriety. It was their holiday.

We meet Frank one morning on a beach near his home in Wells-next-the-Sea, a small village hugging the North Norfolk coast. He has become something of a legend for the hundreds of thousands of people who enjoy small boat cruising, but the renown he now enjoys has not changed him one bit. For a man like Frank, the oceans are simply too good for racing, too beautiful to be places to prove oneself or break a record. He goes out in small boats because he knows that's the best way to understand the sea: 'With proper preparation, it's a way for anyone to meet the ocean on equal terms and experience the deep satisfaction this brings'. You can sense with Frank it's the independence and freedom that still invigorates him. 'We make our own decisions. If you get it wrong you know who is to blame but when it goes right it's absolutely wonderful. To take an open dinghy across a hundred miles of sea, taking the weather as it comes, to see the beauty of a dawn creep across the restless waves, to make a safe landfall and to meet people on the coast for the first time – to me that's the joy of the sea, the real meaning of life.'

LANCASTER SOUND, 1854

JOHN PARKER 1800-n.d.

When Captain Inglefield set sail for the Arctic for the third time, in the summer of 1854, *The Times* reported that he took with him 'a most complete series of the articles used by photographists for depicting nature as seen in the polar regions'. Inglefield had seen the new technique of wet glass-plate photography at the Great Exhibition in London and Archer's *Manual of the Collodion Photographic Process*, published in 1852, explained what he had to do. Sent by the Admiralty in search of the missing Franklin expedition, Inglefield was instructed to sail up Lancaster Sound and as HMS *Phoenix* made her way north, he called in at the small villages on the west coast of Greenland, taking a number of remarkable portraits of the Inuit and the Danish settled there. Just twenty of these glass negatives survive.

On the deck of his whaler *Truelove*, Captain Parker peers at the camera from beneath his brightly polished tarred hat. A whaling master for twenty-seven years, he was captain of *Truelove* for seventeen, a record unsurpassed by any other. Built in Philadelphia in 1764, *Truelove* fell into English hands during the War of Independence when captured as a privateer. She was sold to a Hull wine merchant and later converted into a whaling ship. Over a long career, she made over eighty voyages to the Arctic, dispatching an estimated 500 whales. In 1835 she was part of the fleet trapped in ice in Melville Bay, when some twenty ships were crushed, but she came out unscathed. Captain William Wells described her as 'handy as a cutter, safe as a lifeboat, and tight as a bottle'.

Truelove was the last of the Hull whalers. Though she sailed alongside many of the steam-powered vessels in the 1860s she could not compete with this new technology. In 1873 she travelled to Philadelphia and was presented with a flag in honour of her 'birth' there 109 years earlier. Although there were calls for her to be made into a floating museum, she ended her days as a hulk on the Thames before being broken up sometime in the 1890s.

LONG ISLAND, 2009
ANNE DOUBILET 1947-

Anne Doubilet sits on the beach at Montauk, Long Island, during a shoot for US *Vogue*. Her elegant portrait was created by the legendary photographer Annie Leibovitz. After almost forty years of working in the ocean, Doubilet now spends much of her time travelling, lecturing, and organising activities as a Fellow and Board Member of The Explorers Club and on the Advisory Board of Wings WorldQuest, a nonprofit supporting female explorers and scientists. She has, in so many ways, become an ambassador for the sea.

Massachusetts-born, Doubilet spent her summers growing up on Cape Ann. She smiles when asked about her first ocean photograph. 'It was probably the crashing waves of the North Atlantic, spilling over rocks across the road from our house. I spent hours, not always successfully, in the dark room trying to make a black and white print'. At nineteen, while a student at Boston University, she suffered a near-fatal motorcycle accident that required almost six years of surgeries. 'I suppose I'm a walking miracle', she says. 'I almost lost my left leg. I found my place in the water because swimming is weightless. Now, I simply couldn't be without the sea. It is my place of peace, empowerment, beauty, creativity and challenge'.

She was studying photography when she met her former husband, David Doubilet, already an established underwater photographer. She has since logged over 5,000 dives and photographed in most of the world's oceans, from the Galapagos to Papua New Guinea. Her first assignment was in the Red Sea. She discovered 'the most exquisite paradise you could ever imagine, teeming with corals and anemones and sharks swimming around; polka-dotted stingrays and schools of glassy sweepers; beautiful pink, purple, orange and yellow soft corals gently waving back and forth in the currents'.

That Red Sea reef she describes so vividly is decimated now. She recently chaired a forum in New York, bringing together experts to discuss the crisis in the oceans: coral reefs the world over are under stress, fish stocks have been plundered, industrial waste flows unregulated, whale populations are threatened as never before, a gyre of plastic the size of Texas is blighting the once clean waters of the Pacific. The facts are grim. So dire, says Doubilet, that 'people don't really want to hear it'. But even so, she believes, things are not entirely hopeless. With buoyant awareness of environmental issues, now may be the time. 'I can't find it in my heart to say it is too late'.

WHALE CAY, 1964
MARION CARSTAIRS 1900-1993

Marion 'Joe' Carstairs stands amidst her trophies, model ships, weapons, stuffed fish and leopard skins in her museum on her private island in the Bahamas. One of the twentieth-century's great eccentrics – a game-hunting, cheroot-smoking, cross-dressing lesbian with tattoos on her arms – she drove ambulances in the First World War and later became a champion speedboat racer. She was, by her own accounts, the libertine child of the Twenties: loving fancy dress, dancing, motorcars, cocktails and sex. And she was, without doubt, the fastest woman on water.

Carstairs was born in London in 1900, the granddaughter of one of the Standard Oil trustees. Her inheritance gave her the freedom to live as she pleased, and she channelled much of her wealth into buying and then racing speedboats. 'I have no bent for art or for such accomplishments as one usually associates with girls', she remarked. In Paris she embarked on an affair with Oscar Wilde's niece Dolly, though she would later marry a flamboyant Count to gain better access to her trust fund. She was friends with several male racing drivers, on land and at sea, and she used her money generously to help them. She contributed $10,000 to the building of *Blue Bird* for Sir Malcolm Campbell, who once described her as 'the greatest sportsman' he knew.

In 1934, Carstairs bought Whale Cay, an island in the British West Indies, where in self-imposed exile she set up a fantasy fiefdom of her own. 'I was a leader', she later declared, 'I could do anything I wanted'. The Duke and Duchess of Windsor came to stay for a while, as did a long line of attractive women, including screen siren Marlene Dietrich, many of whom became her lovers. She cleared the coconut groves, built a church and a schoolhouse, and put up a power plant. She rebuilt the lighthouse, dredged up a beach, and created a vast villa complex, complete with a private museum for her trophies. The island was her personal playground, a Neverland in the tropical sun where she would race around on motorbikes, go fishing for sharks and later, if it was her fancy that night, dress for dinner as a pirate. This portrait was taken by Slim Aarons, the celebrated American photographer who made a career out of what he called 'photographing attractive people doing attractive things in attractive places'. Carstairs died in Florida, where she had moved after selling Whale Cay in 1975. Her island home, all but abandoned, is now overgrown, reclaimed by the jungle. The museum is empty.

ISLE OF SKYE, 2009
MIKE PERHAM 1992-

At the age of 17 years and 164 days, Michael Perham became the youngest person to sail around the world solo. At just 14 he sailed single-handed across the Atlantic, in the suitably named *Cheeky Monkey*, but had to sell her to raise money for his ambitious circumnavigation attempt. He brought his 50-foot racing yacht home to Portsmouth in August 2009, after spending 157 days at sea, sailing 30,000 miles and having survived the notoriously rough Southern Ocean. His record is now being challenged by many other ambitious, some may say foolish, young sailors, while the more ungenerous of critics have pointed out that his voyage was neither non-stop nor unassisted. Avoiding harsh winter conditions, he had also opted to transit the Panama Canal. Mike is not too bothered by these questions. His adventure has opened his eyes to the world and he is looking to new challenges.

We join him in Scotland, one winter afternoon, training with the renowned Australian navigator Don McIntyre. In 2010 they plan to retrace Captain Bligh's 4,000-mile voyage in an open boat, when cast adrift from the *Bounty* following the mutiny in 1798. They are raising money for sufferers of motor neurone disease in the process. But for now, Mike's two main goals are 'getting his driving licence and going back to college'. 'Oh, and a third', he says with a smile, 'dinner'.

ENGLISH CHANNEL, 1930
CHARLES NICHOLSON 1868-1954

A pre-eminent yacht designer, Charles Ernest Nicholson stands at the helm of *Candida*. Off his stern is *Cambria* and, just out of shot, *Britannia*, the royal racing yacht, with the ageing King George V himself most likely at the wheel. This is probably the A-class race, fought in a stiff northwesterly breeze, some forty miles off the coast at Falmouth, during the special regatta of the Royal Cornwall Yacht Club in the summer of 1930. Within a year, *Candida* would be converted to comply with new rules to race alongside the J-class super yachts, perhaps the finest that have ever taken to the ocean.

Born at Gosport, the son of a naval architect, he joined the family firm Camper and Nicholson and at the age of twenty-one became its chief designer, a post he filled all his life. A 'rare combination of artist, technical genius, and businessman', he was undoubtedly one of the most versatile yacht architects of his generation. His yard at Gosport became the greatest in England and a second was added at Southampton to keep pace with his imaginative output.

Nicholson produced sailing craft of all sizes, from a 12-foot dinghy for his grandchildren to J-class America's Cup challengers, notably *Shamrock IV* in 1914 and *Endeavour* some twenty years later. He produced clipper-stem steam yachts and diesel motor yachts too, with *Philante*, the largest yet built in Britain. She later became the Norwegian royal yacht. Nicholson was the first designer to see the possibilities of Bermuda rig and in 1921 re-rigged his 23-metre *Nyria*, with a jib-headed mainsail. This brought a storm of protest and some derision in the press, which he rightly ignored. She proved a huge success and would revolutionise the rig of modern yachts thereafter.

In 1939, which marked the end of the pageant of big-class yacht racing, the new 12-metre fleet was almost entirely of his design and construction. By the 1930's ocean racing was also becoming popular and Nicholson was commissioned to produce suitable vessels. Not limited by cost, he produced the incomparable cutter *Foxhound* in 1935, 45-feet on the waterline, and followed her with the yawl *Bloodhound*, which was owned, and raced, by Queen Elizabeth and the Duke of Edinburgh. The doyen of the sailing community, modest and dryly humorous, Nicholson was the technical brain of the Yacht Racing Association right through to the outbreak of war in 1939. Unfortunately, many of his early drawings were burned in a fire in 1941 when his yard at Gosport was almost totally destroyed by enemy action.

PORTSMOUTH, 2009

DEE CAFFARI 1973-

A former secondary school teacher, Denise Caffari changed careers just ten years ago and has since conquered the sport of sailing. She grew up on a motorboat as a child, gaining confidence on the water, while her father shared with her his love of the ocean. She retrained as a watersports instructor on the Isle of Wight and having completed her sailing qualifications she went to work for Mike Golding Yacht Racing. Through a combination of hard work, determination and natural talent, she was quickly promoted to become the skipper of his Global Challenge yacht. She continued her rise to sailing stardom, competing in Caribbean regattas and races such as the Fastnet and the Sydney-Hobart. Leaving others in her wake, she smashed the monohull Round Britain and Ireland speed record. For her portrait, we catch her in a quiet moment, sitting in her sail locker.

In 2004, Dee was the only female skipper in the Global Challenge Race, commanding a yacht with an amateur crew of seventeen all the way around the world. The race was against the prevailing winds and currents and she soon set out to repeat the journey, but this time non-stop and on her own.

In May 2006 Caffari became the first woman ever to complete this voyage. It was an inspirational achievement. In 2007, she began an IMOCA Open 60 ocean racing campaign and this culminated in her competing in the Vendée Globe race in 2008. She finished in a commendable sixth place, becoming the first woman to sail solo and non-stop around the world in both directions.

'Indefatigable, cheerful, resolute and resourceful, Dee is the epitome of a great explorer', ran one commentary, 'and she will – I'm sure – go on to further epic endeavours!' One can be certain of that. Such is Caffari's passion for the sport, she doesn't seem satisfied by this huge success. In 2012 she will compete again in the Vendée and will settle for nothing less than a podium finish. Though this toughest of all sailing races is unpredictable at best, she will certainly give all-comers a run for their money. 'Dee really is a unique person', says the superlative yachtswoman Ellen MacArthur. 'She has achieved some incredible things on the water, but above all for me Dee's just an amazing person, she's fantastic to be around, and I am sure she has helped change the lives of many people'.

NEWPORT, 1937
LADY PHYLLIS SOPWITH 1892-1978

When aviation legend Sir T.O.M. Sopwith's *Endeavour* challenged Harold Vanderbilt's *Rainbow* in the 1934 America's Cup, his new wife, Phyllis, served on the crew as timekeeper. Vanderbilt's wife, Gertie was also a useful member of his crew, keeping the ship's log. It was the first time two women had competed against each other in an America's Cup race. Phyllis returned with her husband to challenge again in 1937, and this unique portrait shows her standing proudly at the helm of *Endeavour II*. It was not a happy year, however. Sopwith was convincingly beaten by the peerless *Ranger* and during the crossing home to England, Captain Williams died aboard from a ruptured ulcer. A year later *Endeavour II* was abandoned on the Hamble River and was sold after the War for scrap metal.

After the death of his first wife, a daughter of Baron Ruthven, Sopwith had married Phyllis Brodie Gordon, a 'bright blonde with pretty teeth', so *Time* magazine reported. Though 'gay and witty on social occasions', Phyllis was no mere trophy wife, but tough, uncompromising, and as adventurous as her husband. She was born in Hyderabad, India, in 1892, where her father was a diplomat and pearl trader. Phyllis wasn't the first woman to race in an America's Cup, but she was one of the most memorable.

In 1886, Mrs William Henn, wife of the owner of challenger *Galatea*, participated in two races against the *Mayflower*, also drawing much media attention. The Henns, unlike any before or since, made their home aboard the boat. As if this wasn't enough to dent their chance of winning, they also brought with them several dogs, a lemur, and a monkey named Peggy who played in the rigging throughout the race. The feisty daughters of Lord Dunraven, Aileen and Rachel Wyndham-Quin, were also afterguard members of the *Valkyrie* challenges. Since then, women have participated as valued crew, fund-raisers, tacticians and skippers in a variety of Cup campaigns. Perhaps, though, Queen Victoria may be reckoned to be the most famous of all. It was she who watched attentively in 1851 as the schooner *America* won the very first race and gave its name to the most famous trophy in sailing. And it was Victoria who, according to legend, first heard the words that have since become its catch-phrase: 'There is no second...'

NANTUCKET ISLAND, 2010

NATHANIEL PHILBRICK 1956-

It's a golden winter's morning on Nantucket as Nathaniel Philbrick gives us a tour of the island. We stop for a moment in the sunshine at Sconset. The Atlantic swell drives in towards the sandy beach, but it's gentle for this time of year. Beyond us, season on season, the cliff top is being eaten by the sea. We continue along heathland, dune and peat bog, through fishing villages long since abandoned to the tourists, past lighthouses and burial grounds, historic homes wrapped in white-cedar shingles, to a new lifesaving museum. There is rich history here at every step. With a guide like Philbrick, possibly the finest maritime author of his generation, it's a special pleasure. 'It's easy to love the ocean', he says, 'It's the only place where I can leave the stories in my head behind; when I return to land those stories always seem burnished and somehow newer; I guess the sea is where I can think without consciously thinking. What a gift to a writer that is!'

Boston-born, Philbrick was an English major at Brown University and took a Masters in American Literature at Duke. He was Brown's first Intercollegiate All-American sailor in 1978 and later that year won the Sunfish North Americans on Narragansett Bay. After grad school, he worked as a journalist at *Sailing World* magazine. Today he and his wife Melissa sail their Beetle Cat *Clio* and their wooden yacht *Marie-J* in the waters surrounding the Island. In the summer of 2010, 'knock on wood', he says, they will be launching *Phebe*, a 38-foot yawl, designed by Bruce Kirby and built by Damian McLaughlin of North Falmouth.

After moving to Nantucket in 1986, Philbrick became interested in the history of the island and its people. He began the Egan Maritime Institute in 1995. He is now best-known for his brilliant writing, including *In the Heart of the Sea*, which told the ordeal of the whaleship *Essex*, the inspiration for Melville's classic novel *Moby-Dick*. It won the National Book Award and in 2007 his next work, *Mayflower*, was a finalist for the Pulitzer Prize. The week we meet, Nat is putting the final touches on his new book – about the Battle of Little Big Horn – and already exploring his next. For now, a busy year lies ahead, with a national tour, lectures and book signings to navigate. And there's his yacht *Phebe*, of course, as soon as she's ready for the sea.

STONINGTON, 1947
ELLERY THOMPSON 1899-1986

Mystic-born Ellery F. Thompson was a fisherman, musician, author and artist. For a number of years he captained wooden trawlers out of Stonington. In the early 1920s, it was said, he ferried the infamous Bill 'The Real' McCoy, out to his schooner *Arethusa* off Montauk. Or so the story goes. As a young skipper during prohibition, it is likely that even if he wasn't in the employ of one of the most famous rum-runners of the day, he would certainly have dabbled in a little 'bottle fishing', a euphemism for netting up the contraband liquor thrown overboard by smugglers with the Coast Guard patrol boats in hot pursuit.

In the 1940s, Thompson and his 50-foot dragger *Eleanor* carried fishery scientists on sampling surveys. 'She was a strong boat', he later recalled, 'a bit like myself, workmanlike in character, with no fancy finish'. In 1947, he won national fame when *The New Yorker* ran a two-part profile on his life. This playful portrait was created by Gordon Sweet as a possible image for Thompson's memoirs, *Draggerman's Haul*, which were eventually published in 1950. But for the Korean War, there might have been a movie too. Henry Fonda and Gary Cooper were considered to play the lead. Meanwhile, quite content, Thompson hung up his boots. He described his home of Stonington as 'a real fisherman's town, where a man can go swinging down the narrow streets, with maybe a couple of shots of rye inside for ballast, and be pointed out as one of the town's leading citizens'. It was the perfect place for the old sea dog.

Thompson remained something of a local treasure. The faithful *Eleanor* met her demise on a mud bank on the Mystic River in the 1950s, when her ageing skipper, battling rheumatism, couldn't keep her up any longer. He painted for fun, until it began to make him money. In the 1970s Mystic Seaport invited him to tie up at their dock and tell stories to visitors. It was here – when not playing his trumpet – that he sold many of his paintings of lighthouses and clipper ships. Thompson passed away in 1987. Charismatic to the last, his grave bears the words, 'Imagine the excitement on the other shore'.

COLDINGHAM BAY, 2010
SIR CHAY BLYTH 1940-

We join legendary mariner Chay Blyth for a walk on a Scottish beach one windswept, winter morning. In 1971, after ten gruelling months at sea on his 59-foot sloop *British Steel*, he became the first person to sail non-stop westwards around the world. It was an epic passage against the prevailing winds – 'the impossible voyage', so said *The Times* – and he laughs when I ask him if he still blames his wife: 'Maureen said, "Well, why not sail around the world the other way?" I had other things to think about, but her words stayed in my mind. Why not, I thought? And, I'm glad she came up with the idea, it was one of the greatest adventures of my life'.

Better, even, than his epic open-boat row with John Ridgway across the North Atlantic in 1966, a feat which made them both household names in Britain? 'Certainly better, although that was quite something too'. As if these adventures were not enough, in 1973 Blyth skippered a crew of paratroopers in *Great Britain II*, taking line honours in the first Whitbread Round the World Yacht Race. Numerous other sailing records were broken and fame followed in his wake. He also acted as skipper for Richard Branson's speed crossings of the Atlantic, before founding Challenge Business to organise a professional round the world yacht race for ordinary people looking to change their lives. He has been a long-time mentor to a new generation of ocean racers – Mike Golding, Peter Goss and Dee Caffari, to name but a few – and was knighted in 1997 for his services to sailing.

FLORIDA, 1954
RICHARD FLEISCHER 1916-2006

This enigmatic portrait, by *Life* magazine staff photographer Peter Stackpole, shows Hollywood director Richard O. Fleischer posing in his new diving suit during filming of *20,000 Leagues Under the Sea*. Fleischer was born in Brooklyn in 1916 and began his motion-picture career assisting on his father's pioneering cartoons, including the loveable sailor-man *Popeye*. In 1954, he was chosen by rival Walt Disney to direct an ambitious reworking of Jules Verne's classic adventure story.

It was the first live-action film with no animation produced by the Disney Studios and their first foray into science fiction. Some of the underwater filming sequences, shot on location off Florida and the Bahamas, were so complex they required a technical crew of over 400 people, including eighty actor-divers, cameramen, sailors and lifeguards. The result, *Life* magazine declared, 'has been the greatest underwater venture in film history'. James Mason starred as the misanthropic genius Captain Nemo, roaming the mysterious depths in his submarine *Nautilus*. His climactic battle with a giant squid has gone down in screen history, so iconic in fact, it has all but eclipsed Verne's novel.

In 1954, *The New York Times* described the movie as 'vivid and crazy'. Though the underwater sequences were innovative, the film left this reviewer wanting more: 'The Disney people have brought within range of their Cinemascope color cameras only a minimum standard assortment of fishes and rays. This could be mildly disappointing to the adults who go to see this film in the expectation of beholding some real submarine phenomena. But the kiddies – those not dedicated to exclusive exploration of outer space – should love every minute of its nonsense. They'll come out of this one wringing wet'.

ATLANTIC OCEAN, 2005
HOWARD HALL 1949-

Legendary underwater film-maker Howard Hall floats into view beside his huge IMAX 3D camera. He's in the middle of a challenging shoot for his epic film *Deep Sea 3D*. His goal that day was to capture footage of sand tiger sharks hunting within a shipwreck lying in about 120 feet of water on the ocean floor off Cape Hatteras. The visibility in the water that day wasn't great, but that didn't matter much to Hall. The IMAX 3D shots he had planned would only work if the camera lens was within four feet of a shark's face. He was going to have to get in close.

'There is almost no shelter for smaller fish except the hundreds of shipwrecks that litter the area here, most of which were merchant marine victims of German U-boats during the war', he relates. 'Enormous schools of fish swarm through the ruptured hulls, dashing inside as large predators like jacks or barracuda rush in to attack. Without this shelter small fish would have no chance. Amazingly, another place they find refuge is beside sharks. They are too small to be of much interest to the sharks but larger predators like the barracuda would be a welcome lunch, so are hesitant to attack. It's an interesting example of symbiosis. And it's also spectacularly beautiful'.

Hall spent almost two and a half hours in the deep waters that day. Two hours of decompression followed. On this occasion they used a seven-minute load of 70mm film, which is two 2,500-foot reels, each weighing about 25 pounds. The film has to be specially manufactured. It costs about $25,000 to process each reel by the time it is printed and transferred to tape for editing. For this movie alone, his crew spent some 1,850 hours filming underwater, shooting almost 75 miles of film. Making the most modern underwater films in the world is a dangerous and expensive business. The sharks in the water, Hall says, are the least of his worries.

BIMINI ISLAND, 1960
PERRY GILBERT 1912-2000

Dr Perry W. Gilbert examines a mako shark at his research pen in the Bahamas. Captured by *Life* magazine photographer Peter Stackpole in 1960, this image was to illustrate a story about new research into 'killer' sharks. 'Since man first took to salt water', the article began, 'no sight of the sea has held more terror for him than the shark ... as many a near victim can testify, sharks can be a gruesome menace wherever water is warm, not only to downed airmen and torpedoed sailors but, in a lesser degree, to every bather, skin-diver or child paddling in the surf'.

The context for this melodramatic magazine piece was a new Shark Research Panel, backed by the US Navy, which had just begun a study of shark behaviour. Dr Gilbert, who was then the Panel's lead scientist, was researching their senses and optical powers, training his ophthalmoscope day after day on freshly-caught specimens. Some, merely anesthetised, were later released in underwater pens for his closer examination. Gilbert and his colleagues spent years trying to develop a shark repellant. While it proved impossible to find one to work on all species, their new understanding of sharks expanded scientific knowledge. Over the years the direction of Gilbert's work shifted. As overfishing and environmental degradation altered the balance of the oceans, he became their champion. He attempted to rehabilitate their fearsome reputation, making them, if not likable, then at least admirable. 'They're just beautiful creatures', he once said. 'They're at the apex of the feeding scale. They have survived for 400 million years. The challenge is to find what has allowed them to do this'.

Throughout a distinguished scientific career, Gilbert edited two books and wrote over 150 scientific papers dealing with almost every aspect of the shark. Equally, he may be well remembered as teacher and mentor to a new generation of marine scientists at the Mote Marine Laboratory in Florida, of which he became the Director in 1967. In an interview given shortly before he died, Gilbert revealed the philosophy that had brought him professional success. 'As a scientist', he wrote, 'I have learnt that there is no substitute for truth, however painful or disappointing it may be'. He continued to feel obliged to put the threat of sharks in perspective for a public that mainly knew them through the *Jaws* movies. 'You're safer in the water than driving to the beach', he often said.

STRAIT OF MAGELLAN, 2006
JAMES DELGADO 1958-

During a preeminent career, Dr James P. Delgado has led or participated in shipwreck expeditions in every ocean of the world, from the deep waters of the South Pacific to the wilderness of the High Arctic. He is most proud of his surveys of the USS *Arizona* at Pearl Harbour and the discoveries of a sunken fleet of atomic-bombed warships at Bikini Atoll, the lost fleet of the Mongol emperor Kublai Khan in Japan, and the 1846 wreck of the US naval brig *Somers*, whose tragic story inspired Herman Melville's maritime novella *Billy Budd*.

Delgado is President of the Institute of Nautical Archaeology, the world's leading organization dedicated to the understanding of humanity's seafaring history through the excavation and scientific study of shipwrecks. Like other great explorer-authors, Delgado is a born storyteller and he shares his passion with a huge audience. He is perhaps most well-known as host of the National Geographic television series *The Sea Hunters* featuring best-selling author Clive Cussler. Delgado enjoys a hands-on approach to preservation, such as leading the crew that restored *Ben Franklin*, a 130-ton oceanographic research submersible originally built for explorer Jacques Piccard, a man who he greatly admires.

'I first saw the sea as a boy visiting California', he tells me. 'The power, the vastness and the curiosity of what lay beneath it fired my imagination. I watched it surge and wash around a wreck stranded on a beach. I have now learnt that the oceans hold the secrets of our past – the greatest museum of the human experience on this planet lies with shipwrecks, resting beneath the seas. The ocean has shaped my life and I feel very lucky to mentor the next generation of ocean scientists. When they ask for advice, I try to show them that success comes to those who work hard while helping others. I like the old sailor's adage: "one hand for yourself, another for the ship"'.

GULF OF MAINE, 1938
STARLING BURGESS 1878-1947

Nautical inventor, yacht designer and aviation pioneer, W. Starling Burgess perches happily on the uppermost fin of a submarine conning tower. The preeminent naval architect of his generation, he is perhaps best remembered for his involvement in the design and construction of the superlative sloop *Ranger*, which sailed to four successive victories in defending the America's Cup in 1937. His father Edward Burgess also designed the Cup defenders *Puritan*, *Mayflower* and *Volunteer*, so it was hardly a surprise that he would also find his calling at sea.

Boston born and Harvard educated, Burgess left university to open his first yard at Marblehead. In 1909 he became interested in aviation and constructed a plane in which he made the first flight in New England. He became the first civilian pupil of the Wright brothers, receiving a licence to sell under their patents. In October 1911 he fitted a biplane with pontoons and became the first to take off and successfully land on water. In peacetime, his design business flourished, turning out many racing yachts that would later become famous. *Rainbow* gave the New York Yacht Club as good a scare as they would get, dropping two races to challenger *Endeavour*, before coming back to win the next four straight. In 1937, Starling took a rising young naval architect named Olin Stephens under his wing, and the result was *Ranger*, the J-class masterpiece. The fastest of all the J boats, she crossed the line a full seventeen minutes ahead of *Endeavour II* in their first race. Those who saw *Ranger* in full sail called her the most beautiful, most powerful, and most destined to win, of any of the America's Cup super-yachts.

In 1930, Burgess had designed the successful Cup defender *Enterprise* for Harold Vanderbilt, employing some radical design features, including a mast made of Duralumin, an alloy commonly used in the frames of airships. For many years, prior to the Second World War, Burgess satisfied his technical brilliance as a consultant for the Aluminum Company of America, helping develop various types of ocean craft including sub chasers, high-speed destroyers and innovative torpedo boats. His phenomenal professional accomplishments, sadly, were not matched by happiness in his personal life. His tempestuous affairs, marriages (of which he had five), and bitter divorces, created untold problems, including bankruptcy, several contemplated suicides and a near addiction to morphine. In all, these were undoubtedly factors in his never achieving the financial success or public acclaim he so desired and, given his brilliance in both yachting and aviation, probably deserved. The author of a number of books, Burgess is also often credited as the inventor of the typeface Times New Roman. He was, no doubt, a man touched by genius.

NARRAGANSETT BAY, 2010

ROBERT BALLARD 1942-

Dr Robert D. Ballard is the world's most famous undersea explorer and oceanographer. With more than 125 deep-sea expeditions to his name, he has been a pioneer in the development of advanced submergence technology including manned submersibles and tele-presence techniques. We meet him on the shores of Narragansett Bay, talking in the early morning light on the pier of the URI Graduate School of Oceanography, where he is a Professor and Director of the Institute for Archaeological Oceanography. A short while later, out of the cold, he shows us around his new 'Inner Space' command centre, enthusing at every step like a proud parent. But he is right to be pleased with its potential – within months it will be possible for researchers and students to monitor, track and share information from oceanographic expeditions and remotely operated vehicles in real-time. It promises a new paradigm for ocean exploration, an amazing window on the underwater world.

In a career that defies a short summary like this, Ballard's explorations have been exceptional. They include the first manned exploration of the largest feature on earth, the Mid-Ocean Ridge, the discovery of hydrothermal vents and their exotic life forms, and the discovery of high temperature 'black smokers' that are responsible for the unique chemistry of the world's ocean. He rediscovered the most famous ocean liner in history, the RMS *Titanic*, the German battleship *Bismark* and many other ancient shipwrecks. Articulate, media savvy and pushing publicity to its best effect, Ballard has attracted a huge following for his work. His ocean enterprise has earned him the National Humanities Medal, the Lindbergh Award and National Geographic's Hubbard Medal, among countless other international honours. 'The key is to follow your dreams', he says with a wry smile, 'and, of course, never get into the thick of thin things'. You know when Ballard sets his mind on something, it's a done deal.

LORIENT, 1976
ÉRIC TABARLY 1931-1998

French sailor Éric Tabarly cleans up having arrived in Lorient after winning the trans-Atlantic race. This courageous master-mariner was an inspiration to those who raced both with him and against him. His influence on a generation of French sailors has been a major factor in their dominance in single-handed and multi-hull sailing. His style and panache won him admirers around the world and his innovations would change the sport forever.

Tabarly became a legend in France having beaten the British to win the single-handed trans-Atlantic race in 1964. There had always been a rivalry between the two maritime nations, but it was the nature of his victory that elevated him so highly. On unpaid leave from the French Navy, he was so bold and fearless a sailor he seemed destined to be the one who 'routed les rosbifs'. His rivals sailed in custom-built yachts while Tabarly took a yacht designed for a crew of eight – the 44-foot *Pen Duick II* – and sailed her alone. He beat the winner of the first edition of the race, the famous Sir Francis Chichester, by nearly three days. President de Gaulle was so impressed he awarded Tabarly the *Legion d'honneur* for his triumph. 'He was this square-jawed, muscular, very fit sailor who always had a swarm of fans and media', remembered a fellow competitor; 'there was a continuous buzz around him, like drones around a queen bee, but he was always just quietly tending to his task at hand'. Jean Guichard took this candid portrait as the hero grudgingly prepared for a press conference. At a later date, when de Gaulle invited him to the Élysée Palace for dinner, Tabarly told him on the telephone he 'could not come as it would be low tide in Brittany, and he wanted to clean the hull of his boat'. Tabarly's priorities were clear.

His intuitive approach to the sea saw him command line honours in sailing races all over the globe, from the Sydney-Hobart, to the Fastnet and the San Francisco to Yokohama Transpac in 1969, leaving course records in his wake. After leading a team in the 1973 Whitbread Round the World Race, Tabarly returned to France with the standing of a movie heartthrob. His admirers followed his every race, the press clamoured to write features about him and crowds lined the piers to welcome him home after each battle with the ocean. His victory in the 1976 trans-Atlantic race with *Pen Duick IV* enshrined his superstar status. He set a new trans-Atlantic record in 1980, crossing from New York to England in little over ten days on the futuristic, 60-foot hydrofoil *Paul Ricard*. At the ripe age of sixty-three, he was voted the most popular sportsman in France.

Tabarly's soul was tied to the ocean. He sailed almost every day of his life. The sea provided him with purpose, a calling, but it can also be ruthless. During a voyage to Ireland to celebrate the hundredth birthday of the original *Pen Duick*, the beloved boat he had learnt to sail on with his father, he was struck by the gaff while changing sails. He was swept overboard to his death.

MONACO, 2009
RON HOLLAND 1947-

We meet Ron Holland at the Monaco Yacht Show. He shows me round the magnificent 190-foot ketch *Ethereal*, one of his latest designs and likely the most elegant and ecologically innovative super-yacht afloat. We stand on the vast foredeck to take a portrait under the sweep of a canopy strung from the boom, taking shelter from the Côte d'Azur sun. On all sides, from the boats nearby, we hear champagne bottles being opened in time for lunch. It is hot and the show is getting busy. We long to escape the marina and go for a sail.

Holland grew up in Auckland, New Zealand, where he was apprenticed as a boat builder and designed his first yacht – the 26-foot *White Rabbit* – while still a teenager. The opportunity to race and undertake ocean passages took him to America where he found employment as a trainee naval architect with the renowned Gary Mull. He returned to New Zealand to help in the construction of an Admiral's Cup yacht and then sailed her to Europe. Back in the US, he designed and built his own quarter tonner, *Eygthene*, which he sailed to victory on both sides of the Atlantic, establishing a reputation that enabled him to set up his own yacht design business.

In 2003, the 247-foot *Mirabella V* was launched, not only Holland's largest design yet, but also the largest single-masted sailing yacht ever built. His studio celebrated its thirty-fifth anniversary in 2009 and he continues to provide hands-on leadership. He currently has yachts being built in Italy and Turkey with plans on the table for a series of superlative new sloops. 'The ocean has been a good teacher over the years', he tells me. 'Originally, I suppose, it was about getting places, and now it's about satisfying my personal curiosity of what we can achieve in design. Sure, we're lucky to be making expensive boats, but the principles are much the same as when we started. We're doing it because we just love to sail. And that's the answer, pure and simple'.

RHODE ISLAND, 1923
NATHANAEL HERRESHOFF 1848-1938

By any standard, Nathanael Herreshoff can be considered the finest yacht designer of his generation, if not the greatest ever. 'Captain Nat' is credited with the introduction of more new devices in design than any other man, innovations that are standard on boats today. The succession of super-yachts that he created for the successful defence of the America's Cup caught the imagination of the world. If that were not enough of a record, it is worth remembering that his first champion – *Vigilant* in 1893, created almost entirely in bronze – was skippered by Herreshoff himself.

Herreshoff was born in Bristol, Rhode Island, and graduated from MIT with a degree in mechanical engineering. He first began experimenting with dynamic high-speed steamboats, but a fatal explosion during trials left him disillusioned by technology and, more significantly, unlicensed as a steam engineer. He returned home and went into partnership with his brother, crafting elegant sailboats for America's elite. Their customers included newspaper magnate William Randolph Hearst, the banker J.P. Morgan, and various members of the Vanderbilt clan. Large budgets meant high expectations, but Herreshoff was able to attract the finest craftsmen in the country who realised his visions for the most graceful and scientifically engineered boats the world had ever seen.

For many, his masterpiece was the America's Cup behemoth *Reliance*, launched in 1903 with a total sail area of nearly 1,600m². His designs were radical. He filed the first US patent for a sailing catamaran, while his 1895 *Defender* featured steel-framing, bronze plating and aluminum topsides. One of his few technical failures – she began corroding, literally dissolving, as soon as she was placed in salt water – *Defender* nevertheless won the Cup race, before being broken up for scrap metal. But the successes were almost too numerous to count. Known as the 'Wizard of Bristol', he designed well over 2,000 craft, producing nearly 20,000 drawings. Between 1890 and his death in 1938, the number of Herreshoffs that won the Astor, Puritan and Kings racing cups, outnumbered the winning boats of all rival designers combined. His America's Cup champions – five in all – were the largest, most expensive and most powerful yet created and were testament to the growing prestige of sailing's ultimate prize.

BUZZARDS BAY, 2010
RICHARD WHEELER 1931-

In 1991, at the age of sixty, Richard Wheeler took to his kayak to make a formidable 1,500-mile solo journey from Newfoundland to Buzzards Bay, arriving safely home not far from where this portrait was taken. Motivated by his concern for the diminishing fish populations of the western Atlantic, he traced the migratory path of the now extinct Great Auk. The early explorers of Buzzards Bay thought them 'marvelous penguins' but their wonder did not last long. A plentiful source of meat and oil, these beautiful, but flightless, sea birds were an easy target and were clubbed to death by the millions in their rookeries off Newfoundland during the eighteenth century. The last two known members of the species, a nesting pair, were killed in 1844, strangled by Icelandic fishermen recruited by a merchant who hoped to sell the skins to collectors. The Great Auk was no more.

To Wheeler, the lost bird became a symbol of humanity's continuing plunder of the seas, a grim herald of the risks that man continues to pose to the ocean environment. Though he was voted *Time* magazine's 'Hero for the Planet' for his efforts, Wheeler saw no reason to celebrate. 'Sometimes I am frustrated to the edge of tears at my inability to make people aware of what we have done to our planet', he tells me. 'The northwest Atlantic embraces a living body as important as the rainforests of Brazil, but which has been subjected to a more prolonged and brutal stress. On the surface we see the same ocean John Cabot saw 400 years ago, but it's not the same. What I hadn't considered before I set out was that the ocean itself could die'.

For Wheeler, our relationship with our oceans is nothing less than a spiritual crisis. His epic journey compelled him to devote the rest of his life to furthering our understanding of the marine environment. For the past twenty years he has remained a modest visionary, one of the ocean's truest champions. Children from Nova Scotia to the Fiji Islands have traced his journey in their school projects while his elegant documentary, *The Haunted Cry of a Long Gone Bird*, has been watched by millions. Admired for its insight and sincerity, it remains a classic in environmental film-making. Its message remains as important now as it has ever been. 'What does it mean to the survival of humanity when we have stripped the ocean of its ability to replace what we have taken away? If the ocean dies, there is no second chance, we are next'.

NEW YORK, 1951
RACHEL CARSON 1907-1964

Rachel Carson's gift was her ability to take dry scientific facts and translate them into elegant, accessible prose. She was, in a sense, a poet who spoke on behalf of the planet – and she was among the first, and finest, of a number of modern writers who urged humanity to consider the health of the ocean. Though her scholarship ignited an international controversy, in the process it gave birth to the environmental movement.

Born and raised in the Allegheny Valley town of Springdale, Pennsylvania, Carson was an avid reader who studied English at university before a biology course reawakened her 'sense of wonder' for the natural world. For a few years she taught zoology at the University of Maryland, continuing her studies in the summer at the Marine Biological Laboratories in Woods Hole. It was there, in her early twenties, that she became enchanted with the enormous mysteries of the sea. In 1935, she took part-time work writing science radio scripts for the Bureau of Fisheries, which eventually led to a full-time appointment as a junior aquatic biologist. She began contributing articles to newspapers and magazines, in an effort to eke out her income. *Under the Sea Wind*, Carson's own favourite among her books, was published in 1941 but it passed almost unnoticed. A decade later her agent circulated a second work in progress that proposed to explore the origins and geological aspects of the sea. Fifteen magazines rejected the material before it eventually found a home at *The New Yorker*, where much of it was serialised. In 1951 the entire manuscript was published as *The Sea Around Us*. It won the John Burroughs Medal, then the National Book Award, and within the year sold more than 200,000 copies. The final book in this superlative ocean trilogy, *The Edge of the Sea*, was completed in 1955.

Success enabled Carson to retire from her job and to speak out more loudly about her concerns for nature. Her long-running campaign against the dangers of chemical pesticides, the sounding alarm of her seminal book *Silent Spring*, brought her praise in some quarters, and bitter censure in others. She was assailed by derision, lawsuits, and fierce personal insults. Despite all this, she remained serene in the face of her attackers – sure of her facts, sensitive and eloquent in her delivery of them. In most photographs her pensive face appears a little sad, but this was true long before she knew that she had cancer. She died aged just fifty-six.

Modest of her achievements, her descriptions of the sea are some of the finest ever written and have inspired a new generation to become advocates for our ocean planet. 'To stand at the edge of the sea, to sense the ebb and flow of the tides, to feel the breath of a mist moving over a great salt marsh, to watch the flight of shore birds that have swept up and down the surf lines of the continents for untold thousands of years, to see the running of the old eels and young shad to the sea, is to have knowledge of things that are as nearly eternal as any earthly life can be'.

OKAVANGO DELTA, 2009
DAVID DOUBILET 1946-

David Doubilet emerges from the water in Botswana's Okavango. For over forty years his images have illuminated our understanding of the hidden corners of our water planet. Along coral reefs, through underwater caves, and from the smallest starfish to the most dangerous marine predators, he has captured it all. He was recently described as the 'underwater Cartier-Bresson'. 'I've got to be happy with that', he says with a smile.

Born in New York City, Doubilet began shooting underwater at the age of twelve, putting his Kodak Brownie inside a rubber bag he'd borrowed from his father's hospital and attaching it to a facemask. 'Unfortunately, we forgot to remove all the air', he laughs, 'so it was like diving with a giant puffer fish'! Since then Doubilet has shot over seventy stories for *National Geographic* magazine. His first was in 1971 when he produced a feature on garden eels in the Red Sea. His most recent assignment was in the Okavango. After working among the sharks and sardines along Africa's coast, he tells me, 'we were excited to come in from the sea to work with crocs, hippos, tigerfish and freshwater gardens that looked like Monet paintings. I was photographing a reed frog clinging to a submerged stalk in the mid Delta region. I lost sight of the tiny fella and turned to my partner and wife Jennifer to ask where it was. She told me to "stand still - don't move" and then took the picture'.

A Fellow of the Explorers Club, Doubilet is a member of both the Royal Photographic Society and the International Diving Hall of Fame. He is a Rolex Ambassador in Exploration and the author of twelve books about the sea. Despite all these accolades, he is not resting on his laurels. The challenge, he says, is to try to redefine photographic boundaries each time he enters the water. It is this ambitious quest for the very best that has made him, without doubt, the world's finest underwater photographer. 'My advice for young photographers is simple', he tells me, 'be true to your passion and interests and have the courage to follow them. But most important of all is to be curious, to ask questions, to want to know why. Even now, every dive is still an adventure'.

PHOTOGRAPHY NOW

The sea is wildly attractive, it draws you on,
you want to set off and see the world.

GUSTAVE COURBET, a letter to his parents, 1851

There's a magic in the distance,
where the sea-line meets the sky.

ALFRED NOYES, *Forty Singing Seamen*, **1907**

I once knew a writer who, after saying beautiful
things about the sea, passed through a Pacific
hurricane, and he became a changed man.

JOSHUA SLOCUM, *Sailing Alone Around the World*, **1900**

DISCUSSION

PHOTOGRAPHY NOW

HUW LEWIS-JONES WITH RICK TOMLINSON, NIGEL MILLARD, JONI STERNBACH AND DAVID DOUBILET

Rick Tomlinson: It all began on a Viking ship. It was sometime in 1979. I was crewing on a replica boat sailing from Norway to the Isle of Man and a few friends were interested in taking pictures. That was probably the first time I thought that I really wanted to be able to take photographs at sea. A short while later, Alistair Black arrived on the island to photograph the famous trimaran, *Three Legs of Mann*. He really was the best of his generation, one of the first to attempt a new kind of yachting imagery. The following year I was lucky to meet the photographer Christian Fevrier and that really sealed it for me. I was desperate to be one of them! But it wasn't until 1985 that I really had my chance to take pictures that people wanted to see. That was on the 78-foot Maxi yacht *Drum* in the Whitbread Race. It was a trip that would shape the rest of my life as a marine photographer.

Huw Lewis-Jones: Are there any particular images that changed your life, do you think?

RT: In the early days I was transfixed by Frank Hurley's photographs from his voyages to Antarctica, in particular his night-time shots when Shackleton's ship *Endurance* was trapped in the ice. In huge seas, or balancing on the yardarm, Hurley really went to great lengths to get his pictures. Frank and Keith Beken's yachting images have defined a golden age of sail, but now it's actually photography below the waves that I find the most amazing. The best in the business has to be David Doubilet. Ten years ago, I was asked to speak at National Geographic and when I arrived in Washington I was shown into the auditorium to prepare. I found the projector and there on the carousel was a whole series of David's slides: magnificent corals, sharks, divers surrounded by beautiful shoals of fish, dazzling in the light – such fantastic photography. I placed my own slide tray on the projector. You can imagine that was quite a moment for me.

It's hard to say what I'm looking for in my marine photographs, what sets them apart. People like dramatic action shots, maybe a small boat battling the giant waves, but as you know it's not all about the biggest 'wow' images. It's often the simple ones that say the most. It's also difficult to say what goes through your mind when taking a shot, it's mostly

PREVIOUS PAGE: A near perfect circle of Barracuda surrounds diver Dinah Halstead in Papua New Guinea, 1987.

LEFT: *Rothmans* buries her bow under white-water, surfing a monster wave during the Sydney-Hobart Race, 1990.

instinct, the split-second. Overall it's patience that becomes the crucial thing. Some images are just pure happenchance. But the overwhelming rest are a result of experience, planning, and having the patience to wait for everything to come together – and then to take that chance when it comes. I love the independence, the not knowing how the day might develop.

HJ: Among so many difficulties facing the photographer at sea, the logistical challenge surely plays a major part?

RT: I agree, yet the challenging logistics often prove the most rewarding part of the job. I think of a recent Volvo Ocean Race when I was tasked with planning a major rendezvous with the yachts off Cape Horn. It's difficult enough to get to the most southerly town in the world – you first have to get to Ushuaia and on to Puerto Williams. You are then about sixty miles from the Cape. We used a military aircraft to take us out. Using a satellite phone we get the yachts' positions and we work out the nearest point of contact and the timing, and just pray that the light will be right. When, and if, we have the pictures, I send them back by portable satellite transmitter. We have done similar assignments in the Fernando de Noronha archipelago off the Brazilian coast and during the Sydney-Hobart Race. I also often travel with a video cameraman and a producer. During the Volvo Ocean Race in 2008-09 we were on the road for ten months, and often in remote offshore sorties, or countries with no technical back up. We packed for all thinkable problems. My photography gear-list was something like this:

- 3 camera bodies – 2x Nikon D700 1x Nikon D200
- Nikon 17-35mm f/2.8 lens
- Nikon 24-70mm f/2.8 lens
- Nikon 70-200mm f/2.8 lens
- Nikon 300mm f/4 lens
- Nikon 16mm f/2.8 full-frame fisheye lens
- Nikon 18-200mm f/3.5-5.6 lens, a great back-up
- Waterproof housings
- Batteries and chargers
- Compact flash cards
- Card readers
- Gerber Multirole knife and tools
- MacBook Pro computer
- Spare hard drives
- 3G computer dongle
- Inmarsat BGAN broadband satellite transmitter
- Iridium satellite phone
- Handheld marine VHF radio
- iPhone
- 12v chargers
- Head torch
- Sea-sick pills

HJ: Work takes you far from home. I like the way the poet Byron summed up leaving harbour: 'The farewell gun is fired, Women screeching, Tars blaspheming, Tells us that our time's expired'. That was 1809, but the moment of departure is still a jumble of activity – the last-minute preparations, the embrace of loved ones, a swarm of journalists and the press. Is that about right?

RT: Yes, it's chaotic but also a soup of mixed feelings. To leave the safety of the land, departing on *Drum*, was a very emotional affair. Just six weeks before we had been upside down, thrown into the water, people were trapped inside. We were moments away from losing a life. And now we were heading out again, out towards the mighty Southern Ocean. It was also the start of a great adventure, the Whitbread had been my single ambition since I was young and now I was doing it.

We didn't win, but that didn't really matter. We had sailed 28,000 miles right around the planet. Coming home was amazing, we had survived, but almost immediately you find yourself confused. I had achieved the only thing that I had ever really wanted to do, so what now? There's always a huge tension release when a boat crosses the finish line, if you have won that leg then the feeling is incredible, a high coupled with the relief that it's over. You're overjoyed to be back with your loved ones, but you also feel the guilt of being away so long and putting yourself in dangerous situations.

The first night in a real bed – one that is still, dry, level, and one you can be in for more than a few hours – that's a proper pleasure. It takes a few days to acclimatise to normal life again. After a few months sometimes it feels like it never happened, just a dream. But often it's back to reality with a bump; you have to sit at a desk for weeks on end working through your images!

HJ: The benefit and curse of digital photography is that that we are able to produce such volume. The more photographers I meet and work with, the more I hear how frustrated they are with the amount of time they have to spend at a computer. Not to mention the time needed to wrestle a huge archive of images into some sense of order. It was Mark Twain who said that 'Photography is 90% sheer, brutal drudgery!'

LEFT: A selection of Rick Tomlinson's favourite images. From top left to bottom right: First night out aboard *Drum* during the Whitbread Round the World Race, 1985-86. This image won the photographic competition for that Leg and was later a double-page spread in *Yachting World* magazine. 'If a single image started Rick Tomlinson's career as a marine photographer, then this is it'; *Mariquita* during the Round the Island Race at the British Classic Yacht Club Regatta, Cowes Classic Week, 2008; *GBR Challenge* bowman Matt Cornwell makes ready for a jibe during training onboard GBR70 *Wight Lightning* off Auckland, 2002; J-class yacht *Velsheda* powers through a wave at the Antigua Classic Regatta, 2001; Vying for a chance to contest the America's Cup, *GBR* sail the Swedish boat *Victory Challenge* over the start line early, forcing them to return, 2002. In the process they scatter the umpire and course marshal boats; *Victory Challenge* sails against *Prada Challenge* off Auckland during the preliminary round robin stages of the sixth Louis Vuitton Cup, 2002.

FOLLOWING PAGE: The world's finest ocean racing yachts rest in the marina in Rio de Janeiro, prior to leaving for Miami on Leg 5 of the Volvo Ocean Race, March 2002.

ABOVE: Nigel Millard's lifeboat action images appeared as a special set of Royal Mail stamps, 2008.

RIGHT: The faces of the Hoylake lifeboat team in 1992. Clockwise from top left: the last shore attendant Stewart 'Tea-boy' Kirk, station mechanic Peter Langley and crewmen Dougie Armitage and Eric Eccles.

RT: That's about right. I can't tell you how great it is to finally escape the computer on my desk. I'm lucky to be able to work on personal projects that can take me sailing to any part of the world. I love the high latitudes and the ice. Having my own stock agency has led to many commissions but the market has changed in the last few years with such a profusion of images available. The real pleasure is to shoot commissioned work that's personally satisfying.

HLJ: Challenging conditions, interesting companions and a good cause. That's your ideal, isn't it, Rick. It makes me think of the work you first did for the RNLI.

RT: Yes, in the early 1990s I was a crewmember of the lifeboat in Port St Mary, Isle of Man. As I was travelling away so much I resigned but wanted to keep involved somehow. Rothmans were sponsoring yachting and they suggested I shoot all the lifeboats around the Irish coast for a book and fundraising material. My friend Nick Keig came with me and we set off with a Land Rover and RIB in tow. The stations were fantastic and we took the boats out into the roughest weather we could get.

People liked what they saw and our shoots were extended to cover the UK. I was using film back then. I had a very simple kit of two bodies and three lenses: a 20mm fixed lens, a 70-200mm zoom and a fixed 300mm. I think I was using the Nikon F3 around that time. Though we didn't get everywhere, we were able to shoot at about seventy stations in all. The RNLI is a tremendous organisation. The lifeboat crews of old must have been the toughest guys ever, to take to sea in the boats they had, wearing the clothes they had. Respect is the only word to use.

Nigel Millard: That's where it all began for me. I wanted to photograph the lifeboat because I admired what they were doing. I started by making a small series of RNLI images for my portfolio. Just one shot was afloat – the majority were at Hoylake on the Wirral as the crew arrived back from a shout. I wanted to catch the moment of release, the relief, the exhaustion and the pride on their faces of a job well done. I also did a series of black and white portraits, some of which are featured here. That was back in 1992.

I made a phone call to the RNLI Divisional Office in Plymouth in 2005. After a few more meetings I began a personal project that has now changed my life. Five years later, I'm a crewmember and my images are used across all media to raise awareness and funds for this amazing charity. They even appeared on a special set of Royal Mail stamps!

Most important to me though, is that I'm part of a cracking team on the Torbay Lifeboat crew. I suppose I've always been inspired by honest, simple things. I remember my first ever photograph, on a family holiday in Scotland. We were near a loch. My Dad had just stopped smoking and had thrown his pipe into the water. But what I really remember from that day is the war memorial we were all standing by. Bravery never goes out of fashion. In some ways that's why the RNLI is such a draw for me. Ordinary people doing extraordinary things – selfless men and women who get out of bed in the middle of the night in a screaming gale to help complete strangers. It's great to know that in today's world there are people like this.

HLJ: There are many hundreds of people whose achievements deserve a place in this book. We could only ever hope for it to be a snapshot of the range of characters that have been inspired by the sea. You could fill a whole book on lifeboat crews alone, brilliant people who risk their lives for the sake of others, hoping for neither fame nor reward.

Equally, there are many famous explorers, scientists and sailors not included here. My hero Captain Cook roamed the oceans long before photography. There is no room for other naval officers, men like swash-buckling Thomas Cochrane, or Admirals Beatty, Jacky Fisher and Jellicoe. No space for pioneering oceanographer Mathew Maury or Robert Fitzroy, Darwin's captain. Of a more recent vintage, I wanted to include sailor and story-teller Tristan Jones, the Australian yachtswoman Kay Cottee, polar mariner John Bockstoce, Guernsey harbourmaster Captain John Allez, the historian Admiral Joe Callo and legendary marine photographer Philip Plisson, to name but a few. Selection is a painful process. I think of naval architect Ted Hood. He won the America's Cup in 1974 skippering the yacht *Courageous*, which he built with his own hands in his Marblehead shipyard. He is another legend that I would have loved to meet during the course of this book. But time was not on our side.

RT: Among modern yachtsmen, all the great names are here – Bernard Moitessier, Sir Peter Blake, Éric Tabarly and Michel Desjoyeaux. I would have loved to photograph more French single-handed guys, the American skipper Paul Cayard, Kiwi Russell Coutts, and innovative designers like Nigel Irens and Adrian Thompson.

ABOVE: The Hoylake crew with their Mersey-class lifeboat *Lady of Hilbre*, 2007. Lifeboats at Hoylake have always needed carriages for launching, due to the tide range over the vast, flat beach. Horses were once used to pull these carriages into the waves. Over the years, tractors have replaced horses and engines on the boats have replaced men pulling on the oars. Though the technologies may have changed, the bravery of these volunteer lifeboat crews remains as strong as ever.

HLJ: Certainly, though we've not been able to include everyone we might have liked, the pleasure in doing this has been the chance to spend time with some remarkable men and women. People whose ocean achievements stand them apart but who are, more often than not, the most modest and interesting people you might ever meet. Welcomed into their homes, we've had the privilege of sharing stories at their table, usually over a glass of wine and a good meal. John Le Carré wrote that 'there is no better company anywhere than those who love the sea'. I would have to agree.

NM: I would second that completely. A few people stand out for me though: Frank Dye, Dick Wheeler and John Ridgway, such fantastic men and all so generous with their time. The whole project has been very inspiring – meeting people across the world who feel so passionately about the ocean. Rick, you've come face to face with some of the most famous names in yachting over the years. Who has impressed you most?

RT: That's a tough question as I'm lucky to be friends with some pretty inspirational people, like Ellen MacArthur, Skip Novak, Ben Ainslie, and many more. It's a privilege to know and to work with them. It can be a strange mix of competitiveness and determination that make these people special. But, if I had to pick one, not the most famous, but certainly the most genuine leader, then it would be the Swedish sailor Magnus Olsson. He's a wonderful guy who just makes you feel better for meeting him. He is sixty years old and just skippered *Ericsson* in his

sixth round-the-world ocean race. I have been lucky to sail with him on four of those and I would go again without hesitation if he called.

HLJ: He's done some amazing sailing over the years. On the historic side, I think of Captain Joseph Warren Holmes, born in Mystic in 1824. Almost completely forgotten now, his epic record as a mariner isn't matched by any other. For nearly seventy years he followed the sea, commanding whaling ships and clippers many times around the world. His father was a veteran mariner too – a fisherman, a smuggler, and for some time a prisoner of war – who lived to be ninety and who kept sailing right up till the day he died. It's no surprise that Joseph took after his Dad, the sea was in his blood. He made sixteen roundings of the Cape of Good Hope. It is possible he went round Cape Horn eighty-four times! But the record for which he was most proud was that no vessel under his command was shipwrecked and no member of his crew was ever lost. An incredible sailor, but what do you think makes a great portrait?

NM: I think that the elements that make up a great portrait are consideration, composition and connection. It's not essential for me to know the sitter but it's really crucial they're relaxed in front of the camera. I explain that I'll be up close as I'm using a wide lens and that I'm not trying to be sensationalist or catch them out. I'm after an intimate, natural, honest portrait. Sometimes we all talk, other times I'll just keep quiet and let them react in the way they want to. The eyes hold the key to any portrait – they show that the sitter is willing or not. Get the eyes right and you have it!

RT: Some people photograph portraits for art reasons, I mostly do it because I'm interested in what a person has done, or what they are doing when we meet. I've always thought it difficult to define exactly what it is that makes photography an art, but for me it's when someone says 'wow, I love that!' I think that is enough.

HLJ: Some of the most beautiful ocean portraits of recent years have been created by Brooklyn-based artist Joni Sternbach. From the beaches of Long Island to Santa Cruz, her portraits of surfers shine with an elegant intimacy often missing in adventurous marine photography. They emerge from the surf soaked but elated. They wait patiently. Sometimes small waves curl around their feet, as if calling them away. Surrounded by wooden flotsam, or at the cliff edge, their poses take on a heroic, perhaps even tribal feel. Yet in their simplicity I think these portraits really capture the spirit of the sea. They are not professionals. They are people who long for the ocean, for the relaxation and joy it provides, for the chance to reconnect.

Even more interesting though is that Joni makes her photographs in tintype, a technique little changed since its invention in the 1850s. It's a wet-plate process: chemicals are applied by hand, exposed and developed before they dry. It's a transient and painstaking technique, but one that can also be magical and energetic. Joni, it suits your subjects well.

Joni Sternbach: I started making photographs in art school, sometime way back in 1972, mind you it was nothing of great interest. I just liked creating pictures, especially of mundane things. I suppose my first serious images of the ocean began in 1999. I started working

with wet-collodion making tintypes, ambrotypes and glass negatives that same year. The wet-plate process requires a lot of gear, so it took a while to get the materials and equipment together. It also took a few years to suss out how to photograph the ocean with such a challenging medium.

In the beginning, my work was concerned with landscape and the remnants of our impact on the environment, so I wasn't really interested in making portraits. It took several years before I had the courage to turn my lens on people. It's an intimate process. I would agree, there's a magic in photographing the surfers. They've expanded my world and even though I've been working on the series for several years, they are the reason I continue. I still feel the same excitement meeting new people and making a photograph together.

HLJ: The whole process is an enchanting one. I enjoyed spending time with you in your studio, preparing plates and going through the stages, but on the beach it's a whole different challenge. Your dark room is a portable tent, set up in the sand. You load your plates into a large rear-view wooden bellows-camera. Covered by a dark cloth, with your tripod balanced in between the rocks and pools of the foreshore, the whole looks as though it has itself emerged from a nineteenth-century photograph. Can you talk us through a typical ocean shoot?

JS: Well, it always begins with madly rushing round trying to remember everything. Like Rick has said, on any shoot there's usually so much kit to bring. I have to make lots of lists – if I forget one thing the entire process might be compromised. When I travel long distances, I ship my

wet chemicals and drying racks in advance and I have friends in different places who store gear for me. I buy all sorts of things when I get there – ice coolers, folding tables, ice packs, beach blankets, plastic bins, distilled water, umbrellas, paper towels and funnels. It's a mad mix of old and new. Looking at my notebook for my next shoot in California, the short list reads like this:

- Metal plates, 65 sheets for a 2-week trip
- Glass, 10 sheets, prep and clean
- Wet and dry chemicals
- Collodion – ether, cadmium bromide, ammonium bromide, potassium iodide, USP plain and 190-proof grain alcohol
- Developer – ferrous sulfate, acetic acid, alcohol, distilled water
- Trays for developer and sodium thiosulfate fixer
- Silver bath with dipper, silver nitrate
- Drying racks x 2
- Deardorff 8x10 camera
- Kata kevlar carrying case
- Lenses, 300mm Symmar and brass 18" Somerville
- Custom-made wet-plate camera-back
- Empty boxes and glassines for 8x10 and full plates
- Folding reflectors
- Tripod and tripod head
- Latex gloves and mask for mixing chemicals
- Coffee filters for chemicals
- Weighing scales and timer
- Sugar for use in developer
- Cotton balls and plasters
- Cupcake holders to weigh dry chemicals
- Darkbox with black cloth and plexi safelight
- Milk bottle for water in darkbox
- Shoeboxes x 12
- Collodion pouring bottle
- Shot glass or developer cup and graduate
- Empty vitamin bottle for used developer
- Gallon brown container for silver
- Fixer containers 1 large, 1 small
- Rocket air-blower
- Business cards and hair-bands
- Bottled wax for cleaning glass
- Gaffer tape
- Big spray and sunscreen...

A usual day depends on whether I'm roaming up the coast in search of a swell, or have already lined up some surfers to meet. Rincon is a break that I have returned to for several years in Santa Barbara. I unpack the van and open up the cart to wheel the equipment down to the beach. It takes us three long trips down a narrow path to get all the gear and distilled water near to the ocean. I set up the darkbox first and then arrange the camera on the tripod. I begin scouting for surfers. I take some time to explain the process and what is required. Cooperation is a key factor in the success of a photograph.

I go back to the darkbox to prepare the metal plate, by pouring the syrupy collodion evenly all over one side. I then gently slide it in a bath of silver nitrate and let it sensitise for at least three minutes. This has to be done immediately. I then secure it in the camera-back in the dark and return to where the surfer is posing and make sure the focus is set. I attach the camera-back to the camera, close the lens, set the f-stop and shutter speed, cock the shutter and remove the dark slide.

I snap the shutter. Exposures range from half a second to three, depending on the amount of UV light, the collodion recipe, the f-stop and speed of the lens. I usually shoot fairly wide open to maximize my shutter speed. After the plate has been exposed it's brought back into the dark, where it must be developed and fixed immediately. The surfer is then free to move. Sometimes they run back into the water, sometimes they come to the darkbox to watch. Once it's developed and rinsed, I bring the plate out to the daylight to fix and finish the process. The plate is rinsed a few times and then placed inside a plastic shoebox covered with water. When back at the hotel, or my studio, I will wash it again and protect the surface with varnish.

NM: It's been interesting to watch you complete such an involved process. It must make you nervous, after so much effort, that the surfer moves at the last moment, spoiling the shot?

JS: I usually only make one image and move on to the next. Sometimes if it's worked really well, then I will ask to do another, but most of my surfer tintypes are one-offs. Collodion remains wet for the entire duration, so anything that touches the plate becomes part of the final image. And because it's a chemical it's quirky and unpredictable, and that lends an element of surprise and ambiguity to each image. I'm always hoping that people will reveal themselves in an authentic way. Even just for a second. It's a case of luck, perseverance and patience. Actually, that's probably the most important aspect in this work. I'm not known for my patience, but I've learnt a great deal about hanging out and waiting for things to happen.

LEFT: Abbey, photographed by Joni Sternbach using the wet-plate collodion process, 4 July 2008; Ed, 4 August 2008; Mary Ellen (detail), 5 August 2008; Three girls with 'Daddy's board' (detail), 29 August 2007.

JS: Absolutely, you have to be open to new photographs all the time, particularly those you think you don't need to take. It's also important to do it for yourself and not to take no for an answer. Find a mentor. I think understanding the world of art and photography through a practicing artist can shave years off the struggle of your career.

NM: I would say it's important to try and shoot the best shot you can, every day. There are always compromises – budget, time, weather, clients, equipment, but so long as you can put your hand on your heart and say you did the best you could in the circumstances then you'll get there. My advice always is to shoot what you are passionate about, whatever gets you going. Look around at other images for inspiration. The most important thing is to get out there and get shooting. If you are learning to swim you have to let go of the side!

HLJ: It is fair to say most of us take a photograph, but only a few people make them. Elliott Erwitt said that photography is the art of observation and the challenge is 'to find something interesting in an ordinary place'. Ansel Adams famously joked that a 'good photograph is knowing where to stand'. Experience pays but great photography is anything but straightforward.

JS: Yes, making is an active word that refers to creativity while taking pictures seems to have other connotations. It's an important distinction. Photography offers a broad spectrum of ways to see the world around us, both conceptually and by chance. Sometimes a great picture appears suddenly, a serendipitous gift. Most other times you have to work really, really hard. Many of my best photographs resulted from showing up consistently.

RT: It's often necessary to focus on a particular type of shot, but being open to what may happen next is what makes the difference. Because most of my work is in sailing, understanding that sport and the consequences of wind shifts, rules, boat behaviour and body language is vital. It helps you to try to anticipate what may unfold. The ocean draws all sorts of people, artists and adventurers. As a photographer, for me it's simply the movement and ever-changing view. One day at peace, the next day a storm, always different.

Most surfers who come over to look at the plates I've just made, agree to participate. The most common response is 'cool', but I've also heard 'wow', 'sick', 'gnarly', and 'awesome'. Surfers have their own language, but I'm encouraged by their reactions. The responses to the darkbox are more unusual. Some think it's a hot dog stand, or maybe I'm selling cappuccino. Someone said a few weeks ago, 'what time does the puppet show begin?'

HLJ: Can you describe one of your favourite portraits?

JS: Sure, I saw Abbey emerge from the water and asked her to pose. She consented. She remained in the water with her board and I asked her to place one end down, so the water wouldn't move her and she would be stable for the long exposure. She struck a pose that was instantly beautiful. She gazed straight into the camera, guileless and open. It was an overcast morning so the light was soft. You can see her eyes, the curve of her torso and hips as she leaned into the board, and she's perfectly still surrounded by water.

NM: Do you ever worry about photographs that you missed?

JS: I try not to think about them, but just today I was remembering a young woman who worked on a ferry in Georgia. She had this amazing head of kinky hair. We sat and talked for a while as we were loading our equipment. I was mesmerised by the way she looked. It wasn't till months later I thought about her and wondered why I didn't ask to take her picture. I was working on landscapes at the time and my mind was so focussed that I couldn't see something right in front of me. My tunnel vision sold me short. I try to be more open to the world now. Broad thinking wins out.

ABOVE: Nigel Millard shooting with his Hasselblad H3D 39 II in its Ewa-Marine bespoke waterproof housing, 2009.

NM: Good images are a mix of pre-production, planning, experience, technical ability, weather-watching, luck, knowing when to press the button, and an 'eye'. People often ask me how long it takes to create a shot. The simple answer is that it can take minutes or days. Planning is essential, as is patience. Rough weather shots need rough weather but if it is too rough, you can't stand up let alone shoot! A typical stormy RNLI shot can take anything from two weeks to six months waiting for the right weather conditions and then maybe just ten minutes or maybe three hours to shoot. You also have to factor in the day-jobs and availability of the volunteer crews. Of course, you can just happen upon rough weather, but that really is good luck.

With so many uncertainties, it's really important to be able to rely on great kit. At the moment I'm using both the Nikon D700 and the Hasselblad H3D 39 II, a whole number of lenses, from a simple 20mm to a 150mm, and stick the whole lot in Ewa-Marine custom-built waterproof housings and rain capes supplied by Cameras Underwater. I aim to put the viewer right into the situation so I use wide-angle zoom lenses, which makes whatever is happening wrap around you and gives the image more dynamism and depth. This means that you have to get even closer, and when you get closer you are going to get wetter. It's also crucial to have a backup. I've lost a good few cameras to the bottom of the Irish Sea over the years!

HLJ: As much as great kit, don't you think a photographer needs a philosophy, an overriding visual or personal goal, to do good work?

JS: Of course, though I didn't start out with a notion to make a body of work based on a philosophy. My work evolves and it's usually sparked off by something visual. There are so many factors that determine if I can even go out and make a picture. Once in full swing of a series that involves the water, I'm checking tide tables daily, weather reports, surf reports, wind direction. It's very much an involved and ocean-connected process.

NM: The one thing that is for certain is that you have to be spontaneous, to be willing to change plans at the drop of a hat. If all the preparation has been done correctly then it leaves you in a state of mind where you can just relax and shoot. Of course, you have to be in the right place at the right time but when you are afloat you have the added issues of standing upright, holding on and keeping a clean, dry lens which can be a lot more difficult than you think. One of the RNLI's favourite images of mine at the moment is of Buckie's lifeboat, taken about six miles out in the North Sea. It's basically just a huge splash of water, a dramatic sea and a flash of orange. When you talk to casualties lost out in a storm, they say you see nothing, then this bright orange thing appears on the horizon, and it's not the sun – it's a lifeboat.

ABOVE: The Buckie Severn-class lifeboat *William Blannin* in heavy seas off the north-east coast of Scotland, 2006.

You may have a grand plan in the back of your mind, but the first element, simply, is to keep the camera still and yourself from being seasick. Some days it's flat calm, other days with the lifeboat you're going out because somebody's life is in serious danger. If the weather is fierce you strap into your seat. There's a time for adventurous photos and a time to be sensible.

RT: Though my assignments are sometimes very similar, it's the ocean that rules what you do. The greatest philosophy in the world goes out the window when you require the cooperation of the weather! Often, you have no control over the lighting on a shoot. If it's a regatta I have no say over the time they start, where they go, how they sail. So in that environment you have to be very fast to react – to try to put yourself in the best place, to guess what may happen. For photographers like me who like to use natural light, you always try and shoot at the beginning or end of the day, but the racing usually starts about 10am and finishes at 4pm. So it's often on the unusual days that you get the best pictures.

A philosophy of working hard is always the best one, and shooting as much and as often as you can. Most of our clients want action and branding, and then more action and more branding. You learn what they like and you look to get as much as you can to best fit the brief. Without it getting too familiar, it's really the question of what might happen next that keeps it interesting.

HLJ: And who knows where technology might take us, or in fact, what problems it may present? 'The virtue of the camera', Brooks Anderson said, 'is not the power it has to transform the photographer into an artist, but the impulse it gives him to keep on looking'. It's a curiosity to see the world in new ways that makes photography such a relevant and immediate language. Though it's hard to predict what's going to happen tomorrow – let alone next week, or even a year's time – what do you think is the future for photography?

JS: In art photography 'devolving' is most likely. When I teach workshops I like to borrow the words of Alan Greene's *Primitive Photography*: 'I was more and more convinced that instead of evolving in recent years, photography had instead been devolving, due to the pressure of outside economic forces. First there was the industry-wide preference for the 35mm camera over large-format, irrespective of the fact that the latter offered more technical and perspective control. Then there was the introduction of the auto-focus cameras. This was

followed by the production of tabular-grain films and multi contrast papers in tandem with the phasing-out of slower conventional films and graded papers. Given these occurrences, the movement towards digital imaging seemed little more than the crowning achievement of downward trends. More than ever before, I realised how completely at the mercy of market-driven forces fine-art photographers really were. I resolved that should the day ever come that manufacturers stopped making what I had always taken for granted – photographic film and paper – I would already know how to make photographs from scratch'. I love the way photography keeps growing but I don't always like the way it changes. Regardless of the medium though, good portraits have the ability to speak to everyone.

HLJ: You make me think of Robb Kendrick, a brilliant photographer who has retreated from the digital age to master old techniques. A sixth-generation Texan, raised in ranch country in the state's panhandle, he tours around with his truck with his tintype apparatus in tow. Quite literally, as his trailer is his dark room and developing studio. Like you, he belongs to a growing group of commercial and art photographers – including gallery stars like Sally Mann and Chuck Close – who have rejected the ease and exactitude of digital photography to experiment, and in some cases to re-learn, the lost art of the ambrotype and daguerreotype.

RT: I've no idea where photography is headed, maybe devolving in some ways, but certainly getting more sophisticated electronically in others. I love the technology and will keep pushing the limits of a camera's capability. And the cameras are getting better and better. It used to be just shutter and aperture combinations but now we have a third control, the ISO setting, which is enabling shots in very low light. The crossover between shooting video and stills is merging with digital SLRs that can shoot both. The speed that images can be seen and transmitted gets quicker and quicker, the Internet demands this. Soon, I'm sure we will see cameras with 3G built in.

NM: There is a place for film and digital. Digital cameras allow ocean photography in locations and conditions that are near impossible to shoot on film. You will only once try opening the back of a film camera in a force-9 gale! One of the issues with digitally created images is the thought that the photograph is somehow 'fake', manipulated or constructed from

RIGHT: The crew of the Tyne-class lifeboat *David Robinson* on exercise in lumpy seas, three miles off the Lizard, 2009.

a number of images rather than being honestly created in-camera. Quite how we will square this one, I don't know. The digital revolution has allowed everybody to take photographs, but that's not to say that every image is a great one. The devil is always in the detail. Technology-wise, I suppose the trend may be for larger and larger file sizes, increased portability, and for reducing prices of certain kit. It would be great when we can have interchangeable sensors – so much better on the pocket and the environment! There is a move to extracting single images from high-definition digital footage, but I think the movie-maker and the photographer use different skill-sets. No matter how advanced technology gets and how inundated with imagery we are, no matter how quickly we race around doing things, a single photograph will always have the power to arrest you, to make you stop and stare.

HLJ Despite the rapid advances in technology, there seems to me something quite traditional about the amount of time still required in modifying, enhancing and working with an image, even though the tools are radically different.

NM: I agree. In real terms, there's not much time difference between shooting digital or film. With digital, you don't waste time waiting around at the lab, you don't get eczema from the chemicals, you don't spend your life in a dark-room and you have much more control over the images, well, unless your clients get too involved! You do, however, sit staring at monitors for hours. You get obsessed with backing up image files and you spend thousands of pounds having to constantly update your kit and software.

I'm not a churn-and-burn photographer. I do all of my own post-production in terms of 'hand-printing': colour balance, sharpening, adjusting light levels on different areas of the image. I choose to do work which allows for the final image to be more considered, even though the work I do is often responding to spontaneous actions. I don't output hundreds of images but will work up just one or two from a shoot. I couldn't ride the desk for days at a time retouching hundreds of images though!

RT: Though some things move so much faster now, there's much in photography that still takes a huge amount of time. Surprisingly, it's a very slow process with digital: every image has to be individually processed. It can be a joy to work with images you

are really happy with, but most of the time for me it's a necessary job to get the pictures out in time.

It's difficult to look too far into the future. Even today I am frustrated because I wanted to take a picture of the America's Cup multihull *BMW Oracle*. As we're speaking on the phone, I'm sitting here in Valencia. I've had two days of waiting around for the wind to be right for these boats to race. But I will quickly forget that and be on to new ideas and opportunities. What would I most like to photograph? Well, my favourite place is Alaska and I have the chance to be there later this year. I would like to be the media crewmember on a next Volvo Ocean Race, to see these boats and crews in their element.

HLJ: So what is the future for the sea?

RT: The sea, well, that's a different story. We have to back off. We've been polluting the ocean and over-fishing for too long. We've damaged the balance of nature so much I fear that we've passed the point of no return.

JS: The future of the sea is, quite simply, the future of the planet. Perhaps the sea will be all that's left. We are all drawn to the water, to the edge of the land. It's spiritually rejuvenating but the ocean itself really needs cleansing. The surface belies what's beneath. On a beautiful day it may look like the sea is so vast that it doesn't need our help, but we humans have done so much damage to it.

HLJ: We need photographers like David Doubilet, for example, who inspire people by capturing the wonder and beauty of the ocean world. But this world is threatened as never before. Photography plays its part in connecting us to the environment, reminding people that the ocean needs protecting before it's too late.

David Doubilet: Sixty years ago, we would stare out across the Pacific and see only the surface. What happened beneath the skin of the sea was out of sight and out of mind. Even the Hollywood vision of the sea was limited to Esther Williams' water ballets or South-Sea 'natives' battling a giant mechanical octopus photographed in a studio soundstage tank somewhere in Burbank. Two simple inventions, the facemask and aqualung, opened a secret window onto the sea. The ability to swim and breathe underwater gave photographers precious time to make pictures. It is imagery that peels back the layers of the sea, exposing a world where light behaves very differently than in air, where creatures and colours exist in places that were unimaginable a half-century ago.

TOP LEFT: David Doubilet on assignment with Caribbean reef sharks, Bahamas, 2008.

LEFT: A sea lion darts through a shoal of salema looking for a meal at Cousins Rock, Galapagos Islands, 1997.

HLJ: Do you recall the first time you saw the sea?

DD: Yes, vividly. I was only two years old. It was the Atlantic Ocean, full of morning light. It's one of my earliest memories. I began making pictures in the green waters off the New Jersey coast when I was twelve. I made a makeshift underwater camera by putting a Kodak Brownie Hawkeye into a rubber bag I'd borrowed from my Dad's hospital, and attaching it to a facemask. The picture was a blackfish that almost looked like a fish. But it was a start, and I suppose it was the beginning of my life in underwater photography.

HLJ: It's a career that has taken you to all of the world's oceans. You've also become a mentor to a new generation of underwater photographers. Who were the people who helped you on your way?

DD: Well, many of my 'ocean heroes' are here in this book. Naturally, as for many of us, it begins with the inspiring Jacques Cousteau. Harold Edgerton was my teacher and his invention of the strobe made underwater photography possible. I would single out Dr Phil Nuytten for his genius for invention, the National Geographic photographers Bates Littlehales and Louis Marden for leading the way, and to the pioneer Jerry Greenberg for his innovations in underwater photography. I've been lucky to meet some wonderful people and to share experiences in the ocean with them.

HLJ: Can you talk me through one of your favourite ocean subjects?

DD: Well, I particularly enjoy photographing underwater with sea lions. One shot that is both a favourite, and rather sad, is the sea lion hunting a school of salema at Cousins Rock in the Galapagos. Most predation underwater is lightening fast, a visual chaos, and it's a challenge to capture the defining moment. For one split second the silver salemas formed a perfect circle around the sea lion pushed to the edge of starvation by an El Niño event, which had driven the larger fish and squid deeper into cooler waters out of their reach. For me this image is a rare decisive moment in the sea.

HLJ: Some argue that photographs can't truly represent the sea. The challenge of how best to reflect nature was expressed long before photography. 'The sea never has been, and I fancy never will be nor can be painted', John Ruskin would write in the mid-nineteenth century, 'it

is only suggested'. One wonders if photographs can ever really capture the joy, the ferocity, the beauty of the ocean? 'To paint water in all its perfection', Ruskin continued, 'is as impossible as to paint the soul'.

DD: Yes, it's difficult to describe the artistic challenge of shooting in the ocean. Compared to the world above the surface, underwater photography is a dark blue world without vistas – at best you can see fifty metres. Here, light has no rules. Some of the most brilliant colours on our planet are locked in the depths of the sea and must be artificially illuminated to be seen at all. But the biggest challenge is time. There is simply never enough time.

The waters of the world have run through my life. Even now, after thousands and thousands of hours in the sea, my partner, Jennifer Hayes, and I enter it with a sense of respectful trespass and great anticipation. Working in the sea is a visual gift that I never take for granted. We have seen great white sharks materialise out of the blue, squadrons of manta rays feeding at night, and mating congregations of a hundred thousand green sea turtles. We have followed the path of war in the Pacific, photographing the wreckage and silent memories.

Every new dive is not just another assignment; it's a small, but contained, voyage of discovery. But for all the joy there is a sense of ever-present doom. Humans have approached the ocean as conquistadors, and what we have discovered we have destroyed, through over-fishing and damaging habitats. Climate change and global warming is all about water. The rising sea level and elevated temperatures that directly affect the polar regions are only part of the problem. The vast amounts of carbon dioxide absorbed by the oceans have changed its chemistry making it difficult for reef-building organisms to survive. Scientists predict that coral reefs may only be a memory by mid-century.

Strangely, the most important images of our oceans were not made underwater. They are the pictures of earth from space. These images put our world into true perspective. I can't think of a better set of words than to quote our friend and colleague in the sea, Sylvia Earle: 'Planet Earth should really be called Planet Ocean'. We have a responsibility to pass it on in good health. If we are to have a future, then we must all realise this. Like anything else we treasure or value in life, we have to offer the oceans our love and respect.

London and New York, 2010

RIGHT: Sea lions play in the sea-grass beds off Little Hopkins Island, Australia, 1986.

THE HEART OF THE OCEAN

They that go down to the sea in ships,
That do business in great waters,
These saw the works of the Lord,
And His wonders in the deep.

Psalm 107:23-24

In its mysterious past [the sea]
encompasses all the dim origins of life
and receives in the end, after, it may be,
many transmutations, the dead husks
of that same life. For all at last return
to the sea – to Oceanus, the ocean river,
the ever-flowing stream of time, the
beginning and the end.

RACHEL CARSON, *The Sea Around Us,* **1951**

AFTERWORD

THE HEART OF THE OCEAN
DEBORAH CRAMER

I live at the edge of a salt marsh, where a river returns to the sea, and time is marked by ebbing and flowing water. The estuary – soft, porous, liminal – belongs to both land and sea, moving from swollen bay to thick mudflat and back again with each turn of the eleven-foot tide.

For me it is a place of beauty, abundance, sadness, and promise. In summer and fall the marsh and dunes are filled with birds – heron and egret, endangered terns and piping plover, black clouds of cormorants, and the occasional red knot resting on its long return from the Arctic tundra down to Patagonia. Occasionally, just after sunrise, or late in the evening, the bay may boil with bluefish or stripers chasing bait, but the winding tidal creeks and thick grasses – nurseries to water that once teemed with fish – are quieter now. Large fish are fewer: so many have been taken. When I first moved here, horseshoe crabs, one of earth's oldest animals, came into the creeks each June, spawning on a high tide during a full moon. Then they were gone, until last year when for the first time in twenty years, the bay was littered with the molts of young crabs.

Huw Lewis-Jones' insightful collection of ocean portraits captures humanity's longstanding relationship with the sea – a relationship both loving and conflicted, undergoing dramatic alteration, and above all, unceasing. Humanity's bond with the ocean begun some 167,000 years ago, when glaciers dried the climate and food was scarce. Early humans living in caves on the coast of South Africa foraged in tide pools for the first recorded seafood dinner – brown mussels, whelks, and giant periwinkles. They came back for more: seafood may have nourished humans on the long coastal migration from Asia to the Americas.

Hominids, perhaps *Homo erectus*, moving west out of Africa took to the sea in boats or rafts at least 130,000 years ago, and humans have gone to sea ever since. Basque whalers and fishermen braved the uncharted Atlantic seeking the fishing riches of New England and maritime Canada. Gloucester, where I live, grew wealthy from the seemingly unlimited bounty of the ocean. The nation's oldest fishing port became one of its busiest, along with New Bedford to the south, and during the heyday of whaling, Nantucket. A rare ambrotype of

ABOVE: A lifeboat
crewman looks out
across the waters of
Ireland's Lough Swilly,
the fjord-like body of
water in County Donegal,
in 2008. The 'Lake of
Shadows', as it's name
in Gaelic translates, is
an area rich in marine
wildlife and steeped
in maritime history.
During the First World
War the lough was
used by the Royal Navy
as a gathering point
for the North Atlantic
convoys. During a fierce
gale, back in 1811, the
frigate HMS *Saldanha*
was shipwrecked here.
There were no survivors,
and some 200 bodies
washed up on shore.

New Brunswick whaling wives, dressed in their finest, hints at just how lucrative the whale fishery became. In contrast are portraits of eight whalers and weather-beaten Sheringham fishermen in their rough working clothes: those who would go out to sea work in a world apart, a world stripped of the extraneous, a world where parasols and lace are out of place. While at sea, the lives of fishermen and whalers are governed by wind, waves, and weather, by the drive to catch fish or whales, and the knowledge that they might never return.

For those whose boats go down at sea, there are those who risk their lives to rescue them.

Nathaniel Philbrick, whose portrait is featured, writes lucidly of the brutality of that life. Today, despite the development of satellite and computer technology alerting fishermen and mariners to approaching weather, fishing is still one of the world's most dangerous jobs. A large plaque mounted on Gloucester's seawall lists thousands of local fishermen lost at sea, including the crew whose tragic story is told in the book and movie *The Perfect Storm*. As long as fishermen take to the water, the list will never be complete.

For those whose boats go down at sea, there are those who risk their lives to rescue them. Nigel Millard, himself a lifeboatman, presents a poignant portrait of a crewman from the Royal National Lifeboat Institution. He looks out over the inscrutable, opaque water, its secrets withheld, the danger unreadable. He is swallowed in his orange survival suit, which will stave off hypothermia for less than a day if he, too, succumbs. We see his back, not his face. The crewman, like so many unsung heroes who risk their own lives to rescue others, is anonymous.

Today, fish are essential protein for more than two billion people and fishermen extract more than 84 million metric tons of seafood from the sea each year. Hanging in the Massachusetts State House in Boston, is a replica of a cod, testament to the Commonwealth's dependence on the sea for its economy and identity. The sea provides, but the yield is far greater than fish alone. The oil and natural gas supplying so much of our energy needs – whose tankers constitute the bulk of commercial traffic entering Boston – are products of the sea. Tiny plants and animals lived and died in the sunlit waves, their remains falling to the ocean bottom where, over millions of years, they were compressed and baked into hydrocarbons. Today they are extracted directly off the continental shelf, in the North Sea and the Gulf of Mexico, and from ancient seafloor now part of continents, in Iran, Saudi Arabia, and Texas. The world continues to look to the sea for energy, harnessing its wind and tides. The sea is rich in this resource: every five days, the Gulf Stream carries as much energy through the Florida Straits as the entire human world uses in one year.

For the time being at least, the ocean absorbs between one quarter and one third of human carbon dioxide emissions into the atmosphere, slowing the rate of global warming. Salt marshes, like the ones behind my home, long thought useless, are more productive than wheat or hayfields. At the sea's edge, salt marshes, kelp forests, seagrass meadows, and mangrove swamps hold half the world's carbon. Carbon dioxide sinks, they are critical to mitigating the affects of a warming earth.

The sea is big business, whether it be fishing, aquaculture, energy, transportation, tourism, or other forms of commerce. New York, Shanghai, Buenos Aires,

LEFT: Half-plate ambrotypes of New Bedford mariners and wives, 1860. From a tiny fragment of a hand-written note, it has been possible to identify, from left: Nathaniel Gilbert, the brothers Samuel and James A. Leonard, G.B. Buckingham, A. Whitman, Jr., George Bulle, Captain W. Reynard and John Manning. The names of the women go unrecorded.

OVERLEAF: Underwater cinematographer Doug Allan follows humpback whales in the Vava'u Islands, Kingdom of Tonga, during the making of the BBC series *Planet Earth*, 2005.

Kolkata – some of the world's largest cities – lie at or near the mouths of rivers. Hundreds of millions of people live within ten metres of sea level, and millions more vacation by the sea each year. With advancing science and technology, the sea is no longer a world apart as it once was – those at the edge of the water are no longer as separated from those out on the waves. When I first went to sea, we had a satellite phone, for emergency use only. I had no computer, no e-mail, and couldn't speak to my husband or young children for three and a half weeks.

For mariners away from home – sometimes for months or years at a time – the Seamen's Mission, founded more than 150 years ago, now called the Mission to Seafarers, still operates in ports all over the world offering aid to those away from their homes and loved ones. Further, the Mission offers SIM cards, cell phones, online chat rooms, and e-mail, helping mariners maintain immediate connections with each other and with their families.

What sends so many people portrayed in this book to sea, what compels so many to leave their homes and families for so long, and so many more to flock to the sea's edge, may be the longing and desire for another deeper connection, one which computers and cell phones can't provide. It's the kind of connection I've felt walking the wrack line, picking up exotic drift seeds

carried in by the sea from other continents, or standing at the shore, throwing a message in a bottle out into the waves, and hoping that one day someone walking a distant beach beyond the horizon will pick it up.

For generations, the sea has called, and comforted us. *The Epic of Gilgamesh*, written some two thousand years ago, describes a powerful king who, grieving for his dead friend, searches for the seaweed that will bestow eternal life. In the opening of *Moby Dick*, Ishmael explains: 'Whenever I find myself growing grim about the mouth; whenever it is a damp, drizzly November in my soul ... then, I account it high time to get to sea as soon as I can ... There is nothing surprising in this.' He goes on to say that all men, 'if they but knew it,' share his feeling about the sea. He describes 'landsmen; of wee days pent up in lath and plaster – tied to counters, nailed to benches, clinched to desks' turning into 'crowds of water-gazers' gathered on Manhattan's waterfront come the Sabbath. Ishmael, the orphan, seeks wholeness from his fractured life and respite from his melancholy, in the ocean.

Who hasn't experienced the renewing, restorative power of the sea, either out on the water or at its edge? Science is now revealing the nature and depth of this ocean connection, a connection perhaps at the source of our longing. Lewis-Jones wisely includes

portraits of scientists in this book, men and women who've spent the greater part of their lives shining light into the dark water, seeking to understand and describe the heart of the ocean. Their findings illuminate the many ways the sea is vital to our health and well-being.

We cannot live without fresh water: the sea is its source. Life-giving rain, yielding fresh water for rich agricultural fields, thirsty cities, and lush forest, comes from the ocean. The water that fills lakes, rivers and aquifers, evaporates from the sea, and will return there, perhaps for several thousand years before once again evaporating and blowing onto the land. The difference between life and death in the Sahel, between high and low water levels in the Tigris Euphrates rivers, and between scarcity and abundance on the islands of the Galápagos, turns on whether rain from the sea is given or withheld. Out on the water, moisture yielding currents are palpable. Sailing across the Gulf Stream, a cobalt river on the edge of the green continental shelf, you can feel the pull of the current and the heat rising off the water.

Scientists have revealed the myriad ways the sea has made our lives possible. Some 3.8 billion years ago, life emerged in the sea, perhaps in a scalding hot spring like those in the depths where new seafloor

is forming. The trillions of living cells contained in the human body hold traces of this marine ancestry. Proteins, essential to cell functioning, contain nickel, copper, and sulphur – remnants of early life at the sea's metal-rich hot springs.

Photosynthesis, the foundation of almost all food webs, including ours, emerged in the ocean. Half the oxygen we breathe is produced by tiny photosynthesising organisms in the sea. The first animal was born in the sea, and we, though we live on dry land, are essentially specialised fish. Their fins became our limbs, their gills our jaws. We still carry the sea within us. Our bodies are mostly salt water and we taste it in our sweat and our tears. I love being out on the bowsprit of a boat at night, surrounded by stars and a sea streaked with the lights of bioluminescent organisms, immersed in our watery beginnings.

Go out to sea only once, and land appears in its larger context – a few dry islands in a planet covered with water. Look at the land closely, and its oceanic origins are revealed: pieces of seafloor built high in the Andes and Himalaya; fossils of photosynthesising marine microbes that oxygenated the atmosphere now constituting bedrock in Australia; the dawn of animal life recorded in seafloor now part of the Rocky

ABOVE: A Papuan fisherman fishes by handline from his outrigger as clouds of baitfish swirl beneath, 2007. These rich, remote waters of Raja Ampat, Indonesia, are the centre of marine biodiversity and a beating heart of the coral triangle.

Mountains and the gorges of the Jiang (Yangtze River). So much of earth's now dry land was once part of the ocean. Life endures here because our planet is continuously recycling itself as ocean basins open and close.

The role of the sea in evolution is pivotal: while continents support only twelve of thirty known animal phyla, almost all, thirty-two of thirty-three, are found in the sea. Less than five percent of the ocean has been explored. The findings of the decade-long Census of Marine Life reveal how much there is still to learn. Its

Today, science explicitly articulates what we have long implicitly understood, that the sea is the source of life.

scientists found one new species after another, and life in surprising sizes and places: on a seamount off the coast of New Zealand, a city of brittle stars, tens of millions of them, linked arm in arm in a swirling current; a 'shark café' in the Pacific, where white sharks gather for six months each year; and in the Arctic, delicate ctenophores living in the -25°C brine left when the sea freezes – the coldest, saltiest water on earth. The diversity of life in the ocean, now and in the past, continues to defy our imagination. Science has revealed, for example, that the number of viruses in the ocean, lined end to end, would crisscross the Milky Way approximately one hundred times.

Yet, just as the ocean's abundance is revealed, it is disappearing, as over the years we have confused immensity with immutability. In the evocative image of the wreck at Sconset a woman dressed in black, presumably a widow, looks tiny beside a large eviscerated boat. Its shattered frame, alarmingly upended in the sand, takes the viewer beyond the picture to attempt to imagine the height and awful power of such a destructive wave. The portrait suggests that the sea is enormous, and we by comparison are small and weak. This is both truth and a dangerous illusion. Hurricane Katrina, the violent 2005 Indonesian tsunami set off by seafloor descending back into the earth, and the earthquake that ravaged Haiti, also triggered by descending seafloor, attest to the destructive power of the sea.

Now, though, we humans have ourselves become a powerful force of nature, as powerful as raging hurricanes, rushing currents or pounding earthquakes. We long for the sea, and our lives depend upon it, yet we are altering its very nature. Exploitation has

removed large ocean predators, restructuring marine food webs. Sharks have lived in the sea for 400 million years. Now many reside on the endangered species list and may not survive us. Scientists estimate that in the last fifty to one hundred years, some ninety percent of the sea's large fish may have been taken. In addition, unabated human fossil fuel consumption continues to warm the earth, increasing the acidity and temperature of the ocean, threatening to turn coral reefs to rubble.

Animal life emerged on earth some 500 million years ago, and since then the planet has gone through five major mass extinctions. We have now precipitated the sixth. Scientists debate whether this new time, increasingly known as the Anthropocene – a time dominated by humans – began when humans extirpated giant kangaroos and woolly mammoths, or when farming replaced hunting and gathering, or when James Watt invented the steam engine. It is in response to painful and preventable loss that Richard Wheeler kayaked 1,500 miles from Newfoundland to Buzzards Bay, Massachusetts in memory of the great auk, a bird brought to extinction through the greed of men. Wheeler's portrait holds his love for the sea and his grief over its degradation.

We have long been called by water. Today, science explicitly articulates what we have long implicitly understood, that the sea is the source of life. The question before us is how we will exercise our dominion. The difference between the mass extinction occurring now, and the others that preceded it, is that ours is self-inflicted. The sea is our lifeline, but we have fully protected less than one percent of its waters.

Our chapter in earth's history has yet to close, the last pages are not yet written. We humans are blessed with consciousness, knowledge, ingenuity, and imagination. There is still time, and hope, that we can restore the sea to health, rebuild its fraying edges, and give true sanctuary to its inhabitants. I feel that hope hundreds of miles from shore, floating in the warm Sargasso Sea, where light falls seemingly undiminished through the clear, peaceful water, where my shadow seems to have no end, and everything seems possible. I feel the promise of life renewed out in the marsh, where with each incoming tide the sea once again nourishes the land.

Whatever we choose, the sea is resilient and will endure. Almost four billion years of earth history has shown over and over again that while species come and go, their tenure here but a moment, the life-giving sea remains.

Gloucester, 2010

RIGHT: A southern stingray soars across the brilliant white sands of North Sound, Grand Cayman Island, 1991.

FURTHER READING

There have been a number of excellent books detailing the innovation and adventure of photography's early years. This list is just a glimpse of some of this literature. From the moment that photographs are created they go on many journeys and this is reflected in the ways that people write about them. The development of photography at sea deserves further study.

• Gerry Badger, *The Genius of Photography: How Photography Has Changed Our Lives* (London: Quadrille, 2007).

• Gordon Baldwin, ed., *Gustave Le Gray, 1820-1884*, with text by Sylvie Aubenas and Anne Cartier-Bresson (Los Angeles: J. Paul Getty Museum 2002).

• Jean-Michel Barrault, *Yachting: The Golden Age* (London: Hachette, 2004).

• Keith Beken, *The Beken File* (Aylesbury: Channel Press, 1980).

• Beken of Cowes, *The America's Cup: 1851 to the Present Day* (London: Harvill, 1999).

• Wayne Bonnett, *A Pacific Legacy: A Century of Maritime Photography, 1850-1950* (San Francisco: Chronicle Books, 1991).

• Pierre Borhan, *The Sea: An Anthology of Maritime Photography since 1843* (Paris: Flammarion, 2009).

• Marie-France Boyer, *Spirit of the Sea* (London: Thames and Hudson, 2003).

• Steven Braggs and Diane Harris, *Sun, Sea and Sand: The Great British Seaside Holiday* (London: History Press, 2006).

• Ian Cameron, *Riders of the Storm: The Story of the Royal National Lifeboat Institution* (London: Weidenfeld and Nicolson, 2002).

• Graham Clarke, *The Photograph* (Oxford: Oxford University Press, 1997).

• William Collier, *The Beken Album* (London: Harvill, 1999).

• Deborah Cramer, *Smithsonian Ocean: Our Water, Our World* (New York: HarperCollins, 2008).

• Deborah Cramer, *Great Waters: An Atlantic Passage* (New York: W.W. Norton, 2001).

• Ian Dear, *The Royal Ocean Racing Club: The First 75 Years* (London: Adlard Coles Nautical, 2000).

• Ian Dear, *The Great Days of Yachting: From the Kirk Collection* (London: Batsford, 1988).

• David Doubilet, *Water, Light, Time* (London: Phaidon, 1999).

• David Doubilet, *Light in the Sea* (Köln: Evergreen, 1995).

• John Falconer, *Sail and Steam: A Century of Seafaring Enterprise, 1840-1935* (London: Viking, 1993).

• Daniel Finamore, *Capturing Poseidon: Photographic Encounters with the Sea* (Salem: Peabody Essex Museum, 1998).

• Chuck Fowler, *Tall Ships on Puget Sound* (New York: Arcadia Publishing, 2007).

• Jean Gaumy, *Men at Sea* (New York: Abrams, 2002).

• Helmut Gernsheim, *The History of Photography: From the Camera Obscura to the Beginning of the Modern Era* (London: Thames and Hudson, 1969).

• Basil Greenhill, *A Victorian Maritime Album: 100 Photographs from the Francis Frith Collection at the National Maritime Museum* (Cambridge: Stephens, 1977).

• John Hannavy, *Victorian Photographers at Work* (Buckinghamshire: Shire Publications, 1997).

• Clifford W. Hawkins, *Argosy of Sail: A Photographic History of Sail* (London: Collins, 1980).

• Mark Haworth-Booth, ed., *The Golden Age of British Photography, 1839-1900* (New York: Aperture, 1984).

• Michael Hiley, *Frank Sutcliffe: Photographer of Whitby* (London: Phillimore, 2005).

• Ed Holm, *Yachting's Golden Age, 1880-1905* (New York: Knopf, 1999).

• Ian Jeffrey, *Photography: A Concise History* (London: Thames and Hudson, 1981).

• Steven Kasher, *America and the Tintype* (Göttingen: Steidl, 2008).

• Robin Knox-Johnston, *The Twilight of Sail* (London: Sidgwick and Jackson, 1978).

• Huw Lewis-Jones, *Face to Face: Polar Portraits* (London: Conway with Polarworld, 2009).

• Gus Macdonald, *Camera: A Victorian Eye Witness* (London: Batsford, 1979).

• Elizabeth Maloney, *Francis J. Mortimer* (Sydney: Art Gallery of New South Wales, 2008).

• Joel Meyerowitz, *At the Water's Edge* (London: Bulfinch, 1996).

• Eric Newby, *Grain Race: Pictures of Life Before the Mast in a Windjammer* (London: Allen and Unwin, 1968).

• Beaumont Newhall, *The History of Photography from 1839 to the Present Day* (London: Secker and Warburg, 1982).

• Philip Plisson, *Ocean* (London: Thames and Hudson, 2006).

• Ranulf Rayner, *The Story of the America's Cup, 1851-2007* (Lancaster: Gazelle, 2007).

• Margaret L. Andersen Rosenfeld, *On Land and on Sea: A Century of Women in the Rosenfeld Collection* (Mystic: Mystic Seaport, 2007).

• Stanley Rosenfeld, *A Century Under Sail* (Mystic: Mystic Seaport, 1988).

• Larry J. Schaaf, *The Photographic Art of William Henry Fox Talbot* (Princeton: Princeton University Press, 2000).

• Grace Seiberling, *Amateurs, Photography and the Mid-Victorian Imagination* (Chicago: University of Chicago Press, 1986).

• Stephen Shore, *The Nature of Photographs* (London: Phaidon, 2007).

• Calvin Siegal and Llewellyn Howland, *On the Wind: The Marine Photographs of Norman Fortier* (Boston: David R Godine, 2007).

• Joni Sternbach, *Surfland* (Portland: Photolucida, 2009).

• John Szarkowski and Richard Benson, *A Maritime Album: 100 Photographs and Their Stories* (New Haven: Yale University Press, 1997).

• John Szarkowski, *The Photographer's Eye* (New York: Museum of Modern Art, 1966).

• Roger Taylor, *Impressed by Light: British Photographs from Paper Negatives, 1840-1860* (New York: Metropolitan Museum of Art, 2007).

• Alan Thomas, *The Expanding Eye: Photography and the Nineteenth-Century Mind* (London: Croom Helm, 1977).

• Rick Tomlinson and Mark Chisnell, *Shooting H2O* (London: Adlard Coles Nautical, 2005).

• Alan Villiers, *The Last of the Wind Ships*, with introductory text by Basil Greenhill (London: Harvill Press, 2000).

• Alan Villiers, *Men, Ships and the Sea* (Washington: National Geographic Society, 1962).

• Mike Weaver, ed., *The Art of Photography, 1839-1989* (New Haven: Yale University Press, 1989).

• Mike Weaver, *The Photographic Art: Pictorial Traditions in Britain and America* (London: Herbert, 1986).

• Robert A. Weinstein, *Tall Ships on Puget Sound: The Marine Photographs of Wilhelm Hester* (Seattle: University of Washington Press, 1978).

• Nicholas Whitman, *A Window Back: Photography in a Whaling Port* (New Bedford: Spinner, 1997).

ABOVE: An RNLI beach lifeguard practising his rescue signals from the shore at Cromer, 2008.

RIGHT: Future merchant marine officers and crew study intently during semaphore class at Leith Nautical College, 1948.

INDEX 100 PORTRAITS

PICTURE CREDITS

Nigel Millard: front cover, 6, 7, 14-15, 44-45, 58-59, 70-71, 94-95, 98-99, 118, 122-23, 138-39, 146-47, 158-59, 162-63, 170-71, 202-03, 210-11, 218-19, 222-23, 234-35, 242-43, 256, 257, 258-59, 262, 263, 265, 274, 278, 282, 286 (top left), 287 (3rd left). **Royal National Lifeboat Institution:** 7 (3rd left & 2nd right), 44-45, 84, 104, 139, 141, 256, 258-59, 263, 265, 274, 278, 282 (top left), 286. **David Doubilet:** 6, 248-49, 266, 269, 279, 281. **Rick Tomlinson:** 7 (top left), 8-9, 10-11, 66-67, 86-87, 111, 250, 252, 254-55, 282 (bottom right), 286 (2nd & 4th right), 287 (1st left). **National Maritime Museum:** 2 (P27532), 33 (left G03631), 35 (bottom right N61697), 80-81 (1915 Nares), 88-89 (G10916 Turner), 109 (P49857), 157 (1964 Larsen), 185 (1864 Cooke), 204-05 (G04258), 272 (P39610). **Museum of America and the Sea:** 38, 56-57, 68-69, 101, 133, 193, 196, 217, 220, 232, 240. **Private Collections:** 6, 7, 12, 26, 28, 33 (top right), 35 (middle & bottom left), 36, 37, 39 (top), 40 (top right, middle & bottom left), 41, 62, 74-75, 92, 106-07, 112-13, 121, 133, 148, 161, 165, 166-67, 172-173, 176, 226-27, 230-31, 282 (2nd & 4th left, top right), 283, 286 (4th left & 1st right), 287 (2nd left & 3rd right). **OTHERS:** Sue Flood, 5, 6 (2nd right), 102-03, 114-15, 276-77, 286 (3rd right); **Beken of Cowes,** 6, 40 (top left, middle & bottom right), 48-49, 212-13; **Carrie Vonderhaar,** 6; **Joni Sternbach,** 6, 260; **Andrea Raso / SGP,** 7 (top right), 151; **Jen Hayes,** 7, 246-47, 266, 287 (bottom left); **National Media Museum,** 7 (bottom left), 30 (middle & bottom), 31 (both), 33 (right, middle & bottom), 35 (top, left & middle), 43, 144-45, 153; **Peabody Essex Museum,** 16-17 (6276), 35 (middle right 20800), 52-53 (12809), 65 (31526), 270-71 (17138); **Pascal Kobeh / Galatée Films,** 18-19; **Scott Polar Research Institute,** 77; © **The Francis Frith Collection, www.francisfrith.com,** 20-21, 35 (top, right); **National Library of Australia,** 22 (an10932811-46), 180-81 (vn3885628); **Royal Naval Museum,** 24, 28, 136-37; **William J. Schultz,** 27; **New Bedford Whaling Museum,** 275; **Getty,** 30 (top), 32, 129, 189, 201, 209, 225, 228-29, 287 (1st right); **Corbis,** 39 (bottom), 54-55, 73, 82-83, 97, 117, 125, 131, 186-87, 198, 237, 244, 286 (2nd left), 287 (2nd right); **Vincent Curutchet / DPPI,** 51, 134-35; **Dominique Charnay,** 54-55; **The Metropolitan Museum of Art/Art Resource/Scala, Florence,** © 2010, 60; **Martin Hartley,** 78-79, 175, 182-83, 194-95, 238-39; **Nate Johnson,** 90-91; **James Honeyborne,** 126-27; **Pascal Della Zuana,** 130-31; **Neil Ever Osborne,** 143; **Fiona Stewart,** 154-55; **Niagara Public Library,** 168; **Jan Söderström,** 178-79; **John Van Hasselt,** 186-87; **Phil Uhl,** 190-91; **Ted Soqui,** 198; **Annie Leibovitz,** 206-07; **Levick,** 212-13; **Ed Luke,** 215, 286 (3rd left); **Caroline Pallett,** 262; **Gregg Miller,** 284-85; **Noah Hamilton,** 287 (4th right); **Tattoo Archive,** 288.
Wherever possible, when there is any doubt, effort has been made to identify the current copyright holders of imagery.

ACKNOWLEDGEMENTS

Huw Lewis-Jones: Thanks to everyone who made this possible, in particular the team at Conway, Liz House our brilliant designer, private collectors, a great number of talented photographers, and my friends and family. And to Kari, with whom I hope to escape to be by the sea.

Nigel Millard: Thanks to wonderful Caroline, my loving family, everyone at the RNLI, and the cracking crew of the Torbay lifeboat.

Rick Tomlinson: I would like to thank my Dad for his great support in all my early sailing adventures that led me into the world of photography, and to my mother who wanted me to get a proper job.

LEFT: Facing a monster wave, adventurous marine photographer Clark Little raises his arm to shoot the shorebreak at Ke Iki on the Hawaiian island of Oahu. This photograph was captured from the safety of the beach by Gregg Miller, 2008.

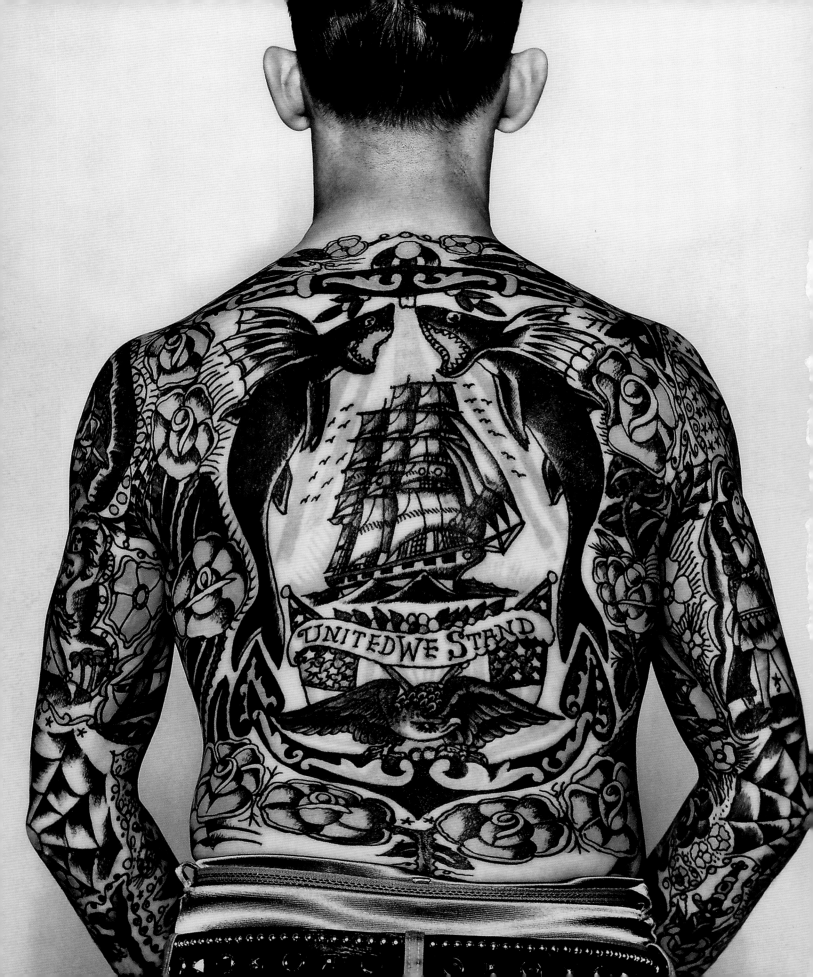